The Bartender's Guide to

Low Carb Cocktails

BarBack Books
Maple Valley

The Bartender's Guide to Low Carb Cocktails

www.LowCarbBartendersGuide.com

ISBN: 0-976-21980-8

BarBack Books are an imprint of:
The American Book Company
Post Office Box 948
Maple Valley, Washington 98038 USA

www.BarBackBooks.com

The information in this book is true and complete to the best knowledge of the author. All recommendations, instructions, and suggestions are without guarantee on the part of the author or publisher. Always serve responsibly. Never serve minors. The author and publisher disclaim all liability in connection with the information in this book.

Every effort has been made to insure that the information in this book is as accurate as possible. The carb counts have been based on currently available data, and may or may not be perfectly factual.

The information presented is not intended to serve as medical advice. Always consult your doctor before changing your eating habits or starting any diet.

Printed in the United States of America

The Bartender's Guide to

Low Carb Cocktails

Contents

None of these have ever worked, but lots of people have asked me....

Is it true you can beat a hangover by....

- Eating peanut butter with Tabasco sauce. *(No, and you will really be a sorry camper when you have all that hot peanut butter stuck to the roof of your mouth!)*
- Chugging a mixture of raw eggs and raw oysters. *(Are you kidding me? No, that won't work, and don't even think about ordering it!)*
- When drinking beer, down several shots of Peppermint Schnapps and tomato juice. *(No, and do you really think you are going to drink that in MY bar?)*

Is it true you can beat a breathalyzer by ....

- Sucking on a penny. *(No, this is not true, and you will probably choke.)*
- Not breathing. *(Of course that makes sense... until you pass out!)*
- Drinking a gallon of water. *(This will not work, and you will probably not make it home to the bathroom in time. Which also means you probably won't be allowed to use your brother's car again.)*

There is one sure-fire way to avoid a breathalyzer every time... call a cab!

The Changing World of Bartending

As a bartender for many years, I have found that people, for the most part, are pretty similar wherever you go. So, it only makes sense that if I notice trends in the nightclubs and casinos here in Seattle, then there is a very good chance that you are seeing the same trends in New York, Los Angeles and Houston. People, I have to tell you, the world of the "carb-conscious" is coming to a bar near you.

You have seen the ads on TV, and read the articles in newspapers and magazines, as the wave has taken over. It is only a matter of time before we will also be dragged, kicking and fighting, into the 21st century. No, I don't mean cellular phones, the Internet, or on-line trading. I mean, the world of carb counters. (Carb is short for carbohydrates.)

Once again, bartending is changing. In the early days, good bartending meant you made a stiff drink, served some of it without spilling it, and turned a quick tip. But, times were hard, and patrons were looking for more. Customers quickly found that they could talk to their bartender much more easily then they could talk to their spouse, boss, or mother-in-law. Before long, bartenders rose to the challenge, adding skills as part time career advisors, marriage counselors, auto mechanics, and matchmakers, to their growing repertoire. (In other words, the number of tricks you can pull out of your hat.)

Now, customers are looking for help in a new direction. At first there were only a few who asked about the carbs in a drink, then a few more, and now it is a regular thing. Good grief! How many bartenders know what a carb is? Do you? OK, well quit panicking and stop handing the customer a glass of water and charging them $5.

Let's make this simple. From what my dieting friends have told me, the new low carb diets reduce the carbohydrate intake (bread, pasta, SUGAR), and increase the proteins (meats, cheese, etc.). Apparently you lose weight as your body is forced to burn the stored fat reserves in place of the usually ingested carbs. Does it work? A lot of people swear by it. As for me, I am still stuck on the four-food groups I learned as a kid in school.

First, they told us that you need a balanced diet, with lots of fruit and vegetables, pasta and meat. That was fine when I was a kid. As I grew older I started seeking new avenues in the food arena.

During my college years I replaced vegetables with a new food group – beer. I was happy and life was good. Who says beer and cold pizza isn't a balanced diet? All the food groups are represented.

A few years later, I started thinking I should slim down a bit. About that time the trend emerged for "low fat" foods. Have you ever eaten a low fat tuna sandwich, or tried to melt low fat cheese for nachos? Yikes! Forget about it, the cheese will burn up before it will melt.

By the way, have you looked at the shelf life for some of those products? "Good through the year 2060." How can THAT be healthy for you to eat?

I can see myself in the future, holding my grandchild, telling him about the "good old days when gasoline was a mere $3.00 a gallon," as we share a protein bar made the year I graduated from high school.

Anyway, back to the subject. The trend eventually changed to reducing meat in your diet. I played along for a while, but *violently* drew the line when someone suggested my sacred Thanksgiving turkey dinner should be made with tofu.

So now, meat is good and sugar is bad. They want me to skip the fruit, and eat pork rinds? I am very confused, and I am sure you are too.

Take heart, things are going to get better. I am here to help you. I went out and bought a truckload of diet pop, seltzer water, soda water, low cal and low carb margarita and sweet and sour mixes, light beer, ultra light beer, soy milk, tofu stuff, non-dairy creamers, sugar-free flavored syrups, and lots of booze. After hours of research and product testing, I have put together all kinds of fun and easy recipes for you, and I have even included the carb counts. To make this even better, I have used items that you will normally either find in your bar, or you can usually find at a nearby grocery store. I have even included a shopping list to get you started.

I have to tell you, some of the testing was a bit brutal. On the bright side, by the time I had five or six drinks everything tasted pretty good. Although I did decided it was time to stop for the night, when I realized I was talking to the alfalfa sprouts as I floated them in a jigger of gin.

Now, just so you have a little more faith in my testing abilities (shame on you, I am a professional), I enlisted the help of several friends and customers. I specifically chose people who do not normally drink diet beverages. I figured that if they thought it tasted good, so would everyone else. After all, what good is it to make up a recipe if no one wants to drink it?

A couple of the more humorous things we found were that the Atkins shakes make pretty good mixers. Who knew? Surprisingly enough, adding more liquor always seemed to help both the flavor of the drink and the mood of the customer. And, the goats' milk shooters were not as big of a hit as I had hoped, but maybe with a little more testing. Let me know what you think.

Once you have the flavor issue figured out, the next point to be aware of is the need for accurate measuring when making these drinks. Especially watch the fruit juices, since they tend to have a lot of carbs. Adding an extra ounce or two can change a low carb drink into a high carb one very quickly.

Besides fruit juice, other high carb items to watch are sweet and sour, margarita, and pina colada mixes, non-diet sodas, tonic water, regular beer, dessert wines, sweet liqueurs, brandies and cognacs.

There seems to be a lot of debate about liquor and diets. From what I can tell, the low carb programs such as Atkins and the South Beach diets allow liquor after the first two weeks. From what I understand, your body tends to burn the alcohol calories before burning extra weight or fats. So drinking liquor may temporarily halt your diet. But then again, if you are too restrictive, then how many people will stay on any diet? You do need to be able to cut loose once in a while.

A couple of other items to keep in mind:

1. **Lower carb does not mean lower alcohol**. A person does not get to order a dozen shots, just because the drink is low carb! Follow your state's normal regulations for alcohol service.

2. What a person is eating, how much, and how long since their last meal will have a significant impact on how they processes and respond to alcohol. Encourage customers to eat while drinking.

There are a few other points to keep in mind as you bravely meet the carb-customer challenge. To help keep you out of trouble here are some important tips:

1) If a woman asks you if you think she should lose weight, **the answer is always, "no."**

2) If a woman asks you if you think she looks fat, **the answer is always, "no."** (Did I really have to tell you that?)

3) If a person asks about the carb count in a drink, and then orders a double cheeseburger and extra fries, it is not acceptable to laugh.

4) When in doubt, say nothing, and just nod understandingly.

5) If a person mentions to you that they are on a diet, it is better to be encouraging. "That's great! Well you look wonderful, so it must be working," is much better than saying, "so, how is that working out for you?" Or worse, "it's about time!"

6) Placing bets on the diet outcome should not be done in front of the customer.

7) It should also be noted that making careless remarks such as "I thought you were just pregnant," to a woman who is not "with child" will probably result in your tires being slashed.

> **Never** ask a woman if is "expecting," no matter how pregnant she looks, unless SHE mentions it to you, or she actually goes into labor in your bar.

8) Do not share horror stories of those who lost weight, and then their spouse left them, they lost their job, jumped off a cliff, or whatever. Keep in mind that people who are on diets are often a little bit grumpy and may be more than willing to take it out on you.

9) Refrain from offering medical opinions. *Playing doctor* on a Friday night with your significant other, does not qualify you to advise your customers.

I love bartending. The excitement, the challenge, the fact that every day is different than the last, and above all, I like to make people happy and want to make lots of money. So, we must change with the times. Unlike the diet fads of the past, the grapefruit diet, the Campfire Girl mint diet, the no fat diet, and the molasses and yogurt diets, I think the low carb diets are here to stay.

Don't worry, there will still be lots of people who couldn't care less about the calories or carbs, as long as they get plastered. You have to love them. And as you serve those liquor lovers and beer guzzlers with a song in your heart and a skip in your step, now you can relax and stop dodging the others. You know who I mean, *the dieters*.

I am giving you lots of tools to help you out. The recipes are easy, the carbs are clearly spelled out, and the ingredients are readily available. Now, go forth and make money!

Hey, wait a minute. I am doing all the work here!

The information presented on this book is not intended to serve as medical advice. Consult your physician before changing your eating habits or starting any diet.

Measuring Tools

Normally, when you make a drink, as long as the alcohol is measured correctly, the amount of mixer is somewhat irrelevant. You fill the glass to look full and call it good. When counting carbs, however, accuracy is more critical. So here is a quick refresher course on measuring and free pouring.

Shot glasses

1 shot = 1 oz

Not all shot glasses are the same.

Most people assume a "shot glass" holds a "shot," but that is not always true.

There are many sizes of shot glasses on the market today. You can't always tell the exact measurement unless you test them by free pouring or with a jigger. Even the name can be misleading. For example, what is commercially sold as a "2 oz shot glass" may actually hold 1-1/2 oz when filled to the rim, and one ounce when filled to the line. And a shot glass labeled "1-1/2 oz" may hold an ounce at the rim and only 7/8-oz when filled to the line.

Don't trust "the line" to mark "one ounce." You will need to measure using another method, such as a jigger. Line or no line, the rule of thumb is to always test new glasses.

Many bars use the "7/8 oz to the line" type of shot glasses, so that when they fill the glass above the line, customers think they are getting "a little extra." Actually, they are just getting the ounce that they paid for. Using these "short shot" glasses, however, can really throw off your measurements for recipes.

Bar Managers

If you are noticing your pour costs are getting too high, or customers are complaining that drinks are not consistent, one of the MAIN reasons may be the way the drinks are being measured.

If your bartenders are using a shot glass for measuring, check to see if the glass really holds a "shot." It may be larger or smaller. Either way, the recipes will taste "off" since the proportions will be wrong. Naturally, pouring the wrong amounts of liquor will also impact your pour costs.

Another possibility is that your bartenders are not free pouring accurately. Please see the next section on free pouring for training information.

Free Pouring

Using a "4 Count Speed Pour Spout" (the most common plastic type), pour some liquor (or use water if you are practicing), into a glass. Count evenly to four as you pour (1..2..3..4). Pour the liquor into a jigger (be sure you are using the 1 ounce side.) Are you accurate? The liquor should bubble up in the jigger but not dribble out. Nor should the liquor be below the top of the jigger. If you have too much liquor, speed up your count slightly and try again. If you are short – slow your count slightly and try again.

Once you can pour a good ounce quickly and consistently, change the glass sizes (rocks, cocktail, bucket, margarita, etc.). You may need to adjust your pouring speed. When you can pour a good ounce into any size glass, change the increments (1/2 oz, 3/4 oz, etc.) Next, try pouring with your other hand.

When you can pour different increments with either hand (and do it accurately, which also means hitting the glass at least most of the time), try pouring using both hands at the same time.

Learning to pour a consistent "4 count ounce" will really help you when you are bartending. You will be able to measure your recipes into any size glass or blender without depending on shot glasses or jiggers. Good free pouring looks professional and allows you to work with increased accuracy, speed and efficiency.

Even if you have never made the drink before, you can do very well using good free pouring techniques.

Some helpful increments to remember

1/8 oz	=	*Quick* 1 count
1/4 oz	=	1 count
1/2 oz	=	2 count
3/4 oz	=	3 count
1 oz	=	4 count
1-1/4 oz	=	5 count
1-1/2 oz	=	6 count
1-3/4 oz	=	7 count
2 oz	=	8 count

Carbohydrate Count

Quick Reference

(8 oz = 1 cup)

Common Mixers

Item	8 oz	4 oz	2 oz	1 oz	1/2 oz
Apple Juice	28.97	14.49	7.25	3.62	1.81
Club Soda	0.00	0.00	0.00	0.00	0.00
Cola	25.67	12.83	6.42	3.21	1.60
Diet Cola	0.00	0.00	0.00	0.00	0.00
Cranberry Juice	36.43	14.49	7.25	3.62	1.81
Crystal Light	0.00	0.00	0.00	0.00	0.00
Grapefruit Juice	27.83	13.92	6.96	3.47	1.74
Lemon Juice	15.81	7.91	3.95	1.98	0.99
Lime Juice	16.46	8.23	4.12	2.06	1.03
Margarita Mix	48.00	24.00	12.00	6.00	3.00
Low Carb Margarita Mix	2.00	1.00	0.50	0.25	0.13
Orange Juice	25.05	12.53	6.26	3.13	1.57
Pina Colada Mix	72.00	36.04	18.02	9.01	4.51
Low Carb Pina Colada Mix	6.00	3.00	1.50	0.75	0.38
Pineapple Juice	34.45	17.23	8.61	4.31	2.50
7-Up	26.00	13.00	6.50	3.25	1.63
Diet 7-Up	0.00	0.00	0.00	0.00	0.00
Sweet & Sour (S&S)	56.00	28.00	14.00	7.00	3.50
Low Carb (S&S)	2.00	1.00	0.50	0.25	0.13
Tomato Juice	10.28	5.14	2.57	1.29	0.64
Tonic Water	21.00	10.50	5.25	2.63	1.31
Diet Tonic Water	0.00	0.00	0.00	0.00	0.00

Some Popular Liqueurs

(Approximate Carb Counts)

Item	1 oz	1/2 oz	1/4 oz	1/8 oz
Amaretto	17.00	8.50	4.25	2.01
Apple Schnapps	8.10	4.05	2.03	1.01
Bailey's Irish Cream	7.40	3.70	1.85	.93
Blue Curacao	7.00	3.50	1.75	.88
Butterscotch Schnapps	10.60	5.30	2.65	1.33
Chambord	11.00	5.50	2.75	1.38
Frangelico	11.00	5.50	2.75	1.38
Galliano	11.00	5.50	2.75	1.38
Goldschlager	11.00	5.50	2.75	1.38
Grand Marnier	6.50	3.25	1.63	.81
HPNOTIQ	11.00	5.50	2.75	1.38
Jagermeister	11.00	5.50	2.75	1.38
Kahlua	11.30	5.65	2.83	1.41
Midori	11.00	5.50	2.75	1.38
99 Bananas	8.10	4.05	2.03	1.01
Peach Schnapps	6.50	3.25	1.63	.81
Peppermint Schnapps	7.40	3.70	1.85	.93
Rumplemintz	11.00	5.50	2.75	1.38
Sambuca	11.00	5.50	2.75	1.38
Sour Apple Puckers	8.10	4.05	2.03	1.01
Southern Comfort	2.70	1.35	.68	.34
Tequila Rose	7.30	3.65	1.83	.91
Triple Sec	11.00	5.50	2.72	1.38
Watermelon Puckers	10.60	5.30	2.65	1.33
Wild Spirit	11.00	5.50	2.75	1.38
Yukon Jack	11.00	5.50	2.75	1.38

Liquor

(Approximate Carb Counts)

Item	2 oz	1 oz	1/2 oz	1/4 oz
Bourbon	0.00	0.00	0.00	0.00
Brandy	4.00	2.00	1.00	0.50
Brandy - Berries	18.00	9.00	4.50	2.25
Brandy - Fruit	18.00	9.00	4.50	2.25
Gin	0.00	0.00	0.00	0.00
Rum	0.00	0.00	0.00	0.00
Scotch	0.00	0.00	0.00	0.00
Tequila	0.00	0.00	0.00	0.00
Vodka	0.00	0.00	0.00	0.00
Whiskey	0.00	0.00	0.00	0.00

Wine

(Approximate Carb Counts)

Item	4 oz	2 oz	1 oz	1/2 oz
Champagne - Dry	4.00	2.00	1.00	.50
Red Wine - Dessert	16.16	8.08	4.04	2.02
Red Wine - Rose	1.64	.82	.42	.21
Red Wine - Table	3.76	1.88	.94	.47
Sake	5.84	2.92	1.46	.73
White Wine - Table	.96	.48	.24	.12

Beer

(Approximate Carb Counts)

Item	16 oz	12 oz	6 oz
Beer	17.52	13.14	6.57
Light beer	6.13	4.60	2.30
Ultra Light Beer	3.47	2.60	1.30

Some Popular Beers

(Approximate Carb Counts)

Item	16 oz	12 oz	6 oz
Amstel Light	6.67	5.00	2.50
Busch	13.60	10.20	5.10
Busch Ice	11.87	8.90	4.45
Busch Light	8.93	6.70	3.35
Budweiser	14.13	10.60	5.30
Bud Light	8.80	6.60	3.30
Coastal Light Lager	5.85	3.90	1.95
Coastal Light Pale Ale	7.20	5.40	2.70
Coors	15.07	11.30	5.65
Coors Light	6.67	5.00	2.50
Corona Extra	18.67	14.00	7.00
Corona Light	6.67	5.00	2.50
Guinness	13.33	10.00	5.00
Heineken	13.07	9.80	4.90
Ice House 5.0	11.60	8.70	4.35
Michelob Ultra	3.47	2.60	1.30
Mike's Light Lemonade	2.67	2.00	1.00
Miller Genuine Draft	17.47	13.10	6.55
Miller Lite	4.27	3.20	1.60
O'Douls	17.73	13.30	6.65
Old English 800	14.00	10.50	5.25
Red Hook ESB	18.93	14.20	7.10
Red Hook IPA	16.93	12.70	6.35
Red Hook Hefeweizen	14.53	10.90	5.45
Rock Green Light	3.47	2.60	1.30
Sam Adam's Light	12.93	9.70	4.85
Sierra Nevada Pale Ale	16.40	12.30	6.15
Weinhard's Ale	17.33	13.00	6.50
Weinhard's Dark	17.47	13.10	6.55
Weinhard's Hefeweizen	12.27	9.20	4.60

Sources:

"Absolut Vodka," *Drinksmixer.com,* <http://www.drinks mixer.com/desc136.html>, (10 June 2004).

"Alcohol and Your Low Carb Diet," reprinted article from www.lowcarbluxury.com, *Low-carb.com*, <http://www.low-carb.com/article-03.html>, (10 June 2004).

"Amaretto Di Saronno," *Drinksmixer.com,* <http://www.drinks mixer.com/desc154.html>, (10 June 2004).

"Atkins Diet Inspires Low Carb Beers," Theresa Howard, *USAToday.com*, <http://www.usatoday.com/money/industries/ food/2003-08-21-lowcarb_x.htm>, (10 June 2004).

"Bailey's Irish Cream," *Drinksmixer.com,* <http://www.drinks mixer.com/desc191.html>, (10 June 2004).

"Baja Bob's Low Carb Drink Mixes," *Netrition.com,* <http://www11. netrition.com/baja_bobs_mix_page.html>, (10 June 2004)

"Beer and Your Health. Calories, Carbs and Alcohol," *Realbeer.com*, <http://www.realbeer.com/edu/health/ calories.php>, (12 June 2004).

"Blue Curacao," *Drinksmixer.com,* <http://www.drinks mixer.com/desc1366.html>, (10 June 2004).

"Can I Drink Alcohol While on Atkins?," *EverythingAtkins.net*, <http://www.everythingatkins.net/atkinsfaqs.html>, (10 June 2004).

"Carb Counter," *Carb-counter.org,* <http://www.carb-counter.org>, (5 June 2004).

**** This is a great reference site for food as well as drink combinations. I found it quite easy to use.**

"Carbohydrate Counter," *Lowcarbfriends.com*, <http://forum.low carbfriends.com/carbcounter/bev.shtml>, (14 June 2004)

**** This is an excellent reference site, and easy to use.**

"Carbohydrate Counts of Common Foods," *Diabetes.about.com*, <http://diabetes.about.com/cs/carbcentral/l/blcarbsA.htm>, (10 June 2004).

**** An excellent reference site, and easy to use.**

"Carbohydrates in Soft Drinks," *Anne Collins Diet, Annecollins.com,* <http://www.annecollins.com/ dietary-carbs/carbs-soft-drinks.htm>, (10 June 2004).

Carol Ness, "Curbing carbs. Dieters belly up to the bar for Atkins-style libations," *San Francisco Chronicle*, March 18, 2004, <http://www.sfgate.com/cgi-bin/article.cgi?f=/c/a/2004/ 03/18/WIGIQ5LTBC1.DTL>, (21 June 24, 2004).

"Chambord Raspberry Liqueur," *Drinksmixer.com,* <http://www. Drinksmixer.com/desc247.html>, (10 June 2004).

"Cocktails," *Low-Carb and Loving it, lowcarbhelp.homestead.com* <http://lowcarbhelp. homestead.com/cocktails.html>, (10 June 2004).

"Crystal Light Product Information," *Kraftfoods.com,* <http://www.kraft foods.com/crystallight/cl_products.html>, (15 June 2004)

"Flavored Rums," *Drinksmixer.com,* <http://www.drinksmixer.com/ desc799.html>, (10 June 2004).

"Frangelico Hazelnut Liqueur," *Drinksmixer.com,* <http://www.drinksmixer.com/desc285.html>, (10 June 2004).

"Gin," *Drinksmixer.com,* <http://www.drinksmixer.com/desc5. html, (10 June 2004).

**** This is a great reference site.**

"Goldschlager," *Drinksmixer.com,* <http://www.drinks mixer.com/desc527.html>, (10 June 2004).

"Grand Marnier," *Drinksmixer.com,* <http://www.drinks mixer.com/desc532.html>, (10 June 2004).

"HPNOTIQ," *Drinksmixer.com,* <http://www.drinks mixer.com/desc1332.html>, (10 June 2004).

"Jagermeister," *Drinksmixer.com,* <http://www.drinks mixer.com/desc535.html>, (10 June 2004).

"Kahlua," *Drinksmixer.com,* <http://www.drinks mixer.com/desc292.html>, (10 June 2004).

"Liqueurs," *Drinksmixer.com,* <http://www.drinks mixer.com/desc29.html>, (10 June 2004).

"Low Carb Beer," *Low Carb Resource.com*, <http://www.lowcarb-resource.com/low-carb-beer.html>, (12 June 2004).

"Low Carb Diets In Review," *Low Carb Resource.com*, <http://www.low carb-resource.com/lowcarb diets.html>, (12 June 2004).

"Low Carb Parties," *Lowcarbparties.com*, <http://www.lowcarb parties.com/index.php?s=tequila&RhRemDetails=0&RhLanguage=en&RhFlashEnabled=1&RhReferer=lowcarbparties.com&RhCountry=US&RhYear=1963>, (10 June 2004).

"Malibu Rum," *Diabeticgourmet.com*, <http://diabeticgourmet.com/forum/counting/index.cgi?read=1782>, (10 June 2004).

"Midori," *Drinksmixer.com,* <http://www.drinksmixer.com/desc303.html>, (10 June 2004).

"Myer's Dark Rum," *Drinksmixer.com,* <http://www.drinksmixer.com/desc506.html>, (10 June 2004).

"99 Bananas," *Drinksmixer.com,* <http://www.drinks mixer.com/desc841.html>, (10 June 2004).

"Peach Schnapps," *Drinksmixer.com,* <http://www.drinks mixer.com/desc191.html>, (10 June 2004).

"Peppermint Schnapps," *Drinksmixer.com,* <http://www.drinks mixer.com/desc1613.html>, (10 June 2004).

"Rumple Minze," *Drinksmixer.com,* <http://www.drinks mixer.com/desc330.html>, (10 June 2004).

"Rums," *Drinksmixer.com,* <http://www.drinksmixer.com /desc2.html>, (10 June 2004).

"Skyy Vodka," *Drinksmixer.com,* <http://www.drinks mixer.com/desc332.html>, (10 June 2004).

"Smirnoff Vodka," *Drinksmixer.com,* <http://www.drinks mixer.com/desc137.html>, (10 June 2004).

"Sour Apple Puckers," *Drinksmixer.com,* <http://www.drinks mixer.com/desc209.htm>, (10 June 2004).

"Southern Comfort," *Drinksmixer.com,* <http://www.drinks mixer.com/desc336.html>, (10 June 2004).

"Stolichnaya Vodka," *Drinksmixer.com,* <http://www.drinks mixer.com/desc326.html, (10 June 2004).

"Tequila," *Drinksmixer.com,* <http://www.drinksmixer.com/ desc24.html>, (10 June 2004).

"Triple Sec," *Drinksmixer.com,* <http://www.drink smixer.com/desc1444.html>, (10 June 2004).

"Vodka," *Drinksmixer.com,* <http://www.drinksmixer.com/ desc28.html>, (10 June 2004).

"Watermelon Puckers," *Drinksmixer.com,* <http://www.drinks mixer.com/desc808.html>, (10 June 2004).

"Whiskey," *Drinksmixer.com,* <http://www.drinks mixer.com/desc5.html>, (10 June 2004).

"Wild Spirit," *Drinksmixer.com,* <http://www.drinks mixer.com/desc806.html>, (10 June 2004).

"Wine, Carbohydrates and Blood Sugar Levels," Lisa Shea, *Wine.about.com*, <http://wine.about.com/library/ weekly/aa061703.htm>, (12 June 2004).

"Wine, Carbohydrates and the Atkins Diet," Lisa Shea, *Wine.about.com*, <http://wine.about.com/cs/recipeswith wine/a/atkins.htm>, (5 June 2004).

"USDA Nutritional Values of Wine," Lisa Shea, *Wine.about.com*, <http://wine.about.com/cs/winemaking/a/usdawine.htm>, (5 June 2004).

"Yukon Jack," *Drinksmixer.com,* <http://www.drinks mixer.com/desc552.html>, (10 June 2004).

Low Carb Shopping List

1. **Flavored Vodkas:**
   Vanilla, Lemon, Orange, Lime, Raspberry

2. **Flavored Rums:**
   Vanilla, Coconut, Raspberry, Strawberry-Kiwi, Cherry, Banana

3. ***Diet* Sodas:**
   Coke/Pepsi, Cherry Coke/Pepsi, Lemon Coke/Pepsi Twist, Vanilla Coke/Pepsi, Lime Coke, 7-Up/Sprite, Orange, Grape, Strawberry-Kiwi, Cream soda, Ginger ale, Grapefruit

4. **Sparkling water** - several flavors. The best ones are those made with only carbonated water and flavoring, no artificial sugar added. (Just my opinion.)

5. ***Diet* tonic water**

6. **Club soda**

7. **Flavored *sugar-free* syrups:**
   Banana, Cherry, Coconut, French Vanilla, Grape, Hazelnut, Orange, Peach, Raspberry, Sour Apple, Watermelon, ***Kahlua***

8. **<u>Low carb mixers</u>:**

Sweet and Sour mix	Crystal Light Lemonade,
Margarita mix	Pink Lemonade, Raspberry Ice,
	Strawberry-Kiwi, Strawberry-
Strawberry	Orange-Banana, Pineapple-Orange,
Margarita mix	Ruby Red Grapefruit

Pina Colada Mix

Blood Mary Mix

<u>Atkins shakes</u>:

Vanilla	Chocolate
Strawberry Supreme	Café au Lait

For other flavors, look in the <u>refrigerated diet section</u> of your grocery store.

Traditional Drinks

This section is made up of a variety of popular cocktails, all of which have been adapted to offer lower carb combinations then the original drinks.

Remember when ordering drinks to be sure you specify the "*low carb version*," or they may be made with the regular full carb recipe.

Absolutely Nutty *(Low carb version)*

Carb Count: < 1
Martini glass, chilled, no ice.
Shake and strain:

1 oz	***Absolut*** Vodka
1/4 oz	***Absolut*** Vanilla Vodka
1/8 oz	Hazelnut flavored sugar-free syrup

Apple Jack Me Up *(Low carb version)*

Carb Count: < 2
Martini glass, chilled, no ice.
Shake and strain:

1-1/2oz	***Jack Daniel's*** Whiskey
1/8 oz	Apple flavored sugar-free syrup
1/2 oz	Apple juice

Apple Mint *(Low carb version)*

Carb Count: < 2
Martini glass, chilled, no ice.
Shake and strain:

1-1/2oz	Vodka
1/8 oz	Apple flavored sugar-free syrup
1/8 oz	Crème de Menthe flavored sugar-free syrup
1/2 oz	Apple juice

Apple Slammer *(Low carb version)*

Carb Count: < 1
Bucket glass, fill with ice.

1 oz	Vodka
1/8 oz	Sour Apple flavored sugar-free syrup
1 oz	Sparkling water or club soda

Fill the glass with diet 7-Up.

Bahama Breeze *(Low carb version)*

Carb Count: < 1.5
Champagne flute, chilled.

1 oz	Dry champagne (chilled)
2 oz	White wine (chilled)
1 oz	Sparkling water (chilled)
1/8 oz	Cherry flavored sugar-free syrup
1/8 oz	Banana flavored sugar-free syrup

Banana Creamsickle *(Low carb version)*

Carb Count: < 2
Bucket glass, fill with ice.
Shake and strain:

1 oz	Banana Rum
1/8 oz	Orange flavored sugar-free syrup

Fill the glass with Atkins Advantage Vanilla or Strawberry Supreme Shake.

Bay Breeze *(Low carb version)*

Carb Count: < 4.5
Bucket glass, fill with ice.

1 oz	Vodka
1/2 oz	Pineapple juice
1/2 oz	Cranberry juice

Fill the glass with sparkling water or diet 7-Up.

Beach Babe *(Low carb version)*

Carb Count: < 2.1
Martini glass, chilled, no ice.
Shake and strain:

1-1/2 oz	Pineapple-Coconut Rum
1/8 oz	Watermelon flavored sugar-free syrup
1/8 oz	Banana flavored sugar-free syrup
1/4 oz	Pineapple juice
1/4 oz	Orange juice

Beach Ball *(Low carb version)*

Carb Count: < 2.6
Martini glass, chilled, no ice.
Shake and strain:

1 oz	Vodka
1/2 oz	***Malibu*** Coconut Rum
1/8 oz	Watermelon flavored sugar-free syrup
1/2 oz	Pineapple juice

Beam and Coke *(Low carb version)*

Carb Count: < 1
Bucket glass, fill with ice.

1 oz ***Jim Beam*** Bourbon

Fill the glass with diet Coke.

Beautiful *(Low carb version)*

Carb Count: < 5.50
Brandy snifter, warmed.

1/2 oz	***Grand Marnier***
1 oz	***Courvoisier*** Cognac

Berry Beautiful *(Low carb version)*

Carb Count: < 5.50
Brandy snifter, warmed.

1/4 oz	***Chambord***
1-1/4 oz	***Courvoisier*** Cognac

Big Freak'n Deal ***(BFD)*** ***(Low carb version)***

Carb Count: < 1
Martini glass, chilled, no ice.
Shake and strain:

1 oz Gin
1 oz Rum
1/2 oz Dry Vermouth

Black Jamaican

Carb Count: < 5.75
Rocks glass, fill with ice.

1 oz ***Myers'*** Rum
1/2 oz ***Kahlua***

Black Russian

Carb Count: < 5.75
Rocks glass, fill with ice.

1 oz Vodka
1/2 oz ***Kahlua***

Black Vanilla Russian

Carb Count: < 5.75
Rocks glass, fill with ice.

1 oz Vanilla Vodka
1/2 oz ***Kahlua***

> Anheuser-Busch has one of the largest herds of Clydesdale horses in the world - over 250.

Bloody Maria *(Low carb version)*

Carb Count: < 2

In a mixing glass, 1/3 filled with ice, combine:

1 oz	Tequila
2-3 dashes	Salt and pepper
2 dashes	Wocerstershire Sauce
2 dashes	Red Tabasco
2 dashes	Green Tabasco *(*** HOT***)*
1 oz	Tomato juice
Splash	Lime juice

Shake thoroughly, then strain into a bucket glass filled with ice. The rim may be salted if desired.

Bloody Mary *(Low carb version)*

Carb Count: < 2

In a mixing glass, 1/3 filled with ice, combine:

1 oz	Vodka
2-3 dashes	Salt and pepper
2 dashes	Wocerstershire Sauce
2 dashes	Red Tabasco
2 dashes	Green Tabasco *(*** HOT***)*
1 oz	Tomato juice
Splash	Lime juice

Shake thoroughly, then strain into a bucket glass filled with ice. The rim may be salted if desired.

Blue Fish *(Low carb version)*

Carb Count: < 3

Hurricane glass, fill with ice. Shake and strain:

2 oz	***Absolut Citron*** Vodka
1/8 oz	Orange flavored sugar-free syrup
1 oz	Low carb sweet and sour
1 oz	Sparkling water or diet 7-Up
2 drops	Blue food coloring
1 oz	White cranberry juice

Blue Hawaiian *(Low carb version)*

Carb Count: < 3.75

Tall glass, fill with ice.

1 oz	Rum
1/2 oz	Lemon Vodka
1/8 oz	Orange flavored sugar-free syrup
2 oz	Low carb sweet and sour
1/2 oz	Sparkling water
2 drops	Blue food coloring
1 oz	Pineapple juice

Overheard in the bar

Who says there is no such thing as common sense?

"So I said to the IRS agent..."

"So I lied. What are you going to do about it, put me in jail?" (Come to think of it, I haven't seen Billy-Bob for a while now.)

"Are we done? Good. I'm glad you didn't ask about my off-shore bank accounts."

Blue Hypno Goose *(Low carb version)*

Carb Count: < 7

Martini glass, chilled. Shake and strain:

1 oz	***Grey Goose*** Vodka
1/2 oz	Lemon Vodka
1/2 oz	***HPNOTIC***
2 oz	Low carb sweet and sour
1/2 oz	Sparkling water
Splash	Pineapple juice

Blue Suede *(Low carb version)*

Carb Count: < 3

Martini glass, chilled, no ice.

Shake and strain:

1oz	***Malibu*** Coconut Rum
1/2 oz	Vodka
1/8 oz	Blueberry flavored sugar-free syrup
1/8 oz	Orange flavored sugar-free syrup
Splash	Lime juice
1/2 oz	Pineapple juice

Bourbon 'n Tonic *(Low carb version)*

Carb Count: < 1

Bucket glass, fill with ice.

1 oz Bourbon

Fill the glass with **diet** tonic water.

Brass Monkey *(Low carb version)*

Carb Count: < 1
Bucket glass, fill with ice.

1/2 oz Vodka
1/2 oz Rum

Fill the glass with Crystal Light Pineapple-Orange drink.

Brass Monkey #2 *(Low carb version)*

Carb Count: < 3.25
Bucket glass, fill with ice.

1/2 oz Vodka
1/2 oz Rum
1 oz Orange juice

Fill the glass with diet orange soda.

Brave Bull

Carb Count: < 5.75
Rocks glass, fill with ice.

1 oz Tequila
1/2 oz ***Kahlua***

Butterscoth Pudding *(Low carb version)*

Carb Count: < 7.25
Rocks glass, fill with ice.

1/4 oz ***Bailey's*** Irish Cream
3/4 oz Vanilla Vodka
1/2 oz Butterscotch Schnapps

Fill the glass with diet Coke.

Buttery Nipple Cocktail *(Low carb version)*

Carb Count: < 7.25
Rocks glass, fill with ice.

1/4 oz ***Bailey's*** Irish Cream
3/4 oz Vanilla Vodka
1/2 oz Butterscotch Schnapps

Fill the glass with club soda.

Cactus Cooler *(Low carb version)*

Carb Count: < 3.25
Bucket glass, fill with ice.

1 oz Tequila
1 oz Orange juice

Nearly fill the glass with diet orange soda and sparkling water. Top with 1/8 oz French Vanilla flavored sugar-free syrup.

Canyon Redneck *(Low carb version)*

Carb Count: < 1
Bucket glass, fill with ice.

1-1/2 oz Bourbon
1/8 oz Peppermint flavored sugar-free syrup.

Fill the glass with sparkling water.

Cape Cod *(Low carb version)*

Carb Count: < 3.75
Bucket glass, fill with ice.

1 oz Vodka
1 oz Cranberry juice

Fill the glass with Crystal Light Raspberry Ice drink, sparkling water, or diet 7-Up.

Captain Coke *(Low carb version)*

Carb Count: < 1
Bucket glass, fill with ice.

1 oz ***Captain Morgan*** Rum

Fill the glass with diet Coke.

Captain Cream *(Low carb version)*

Carb Count: < 1
Bucket glass, fill with ice.

1 oz ***Captain Morgan*** Rum

Fill the glass with diet cream soda.

Captain 7 *(Low carb version)*

Carb Count: < 1
Bucket glass, fill with ice.

1 oz ***Captain Morgan*** Rum

Fill the glass with diet 7-Up.

Caramel Apple Slammer *(Low carb version)*

Carb Count: < 1
Bucket glass, fill with ice.

1 oz Vodka
1/8 oz Apple flavored sugar-free syrup
1/8 oz Caramel flavored sugar-free syrup
1 oz Sparkling water

Fill the glass with diet 7-Up or diet cream soda.

Caramel Berry Blitz *(Low carb version)*

Carb Count: < 2
Bucket glass, fill with ice.
Shake and strain:

1 oz Vodka
1/8 oz Caramel flavored sugar-free syrup

Fill the glass with Atkins Advantage Strawberry Shake.

Caramel Berry Boost *(Low carb version)*

Carb Count: < 2
Bucket glass, fill with ice.
Shake and strain:

1 oz Rum
1/8 oz Caramel flavored sugar-free syrup

Fill the glass with Atkins Advantage Strawberry Shake.

Caramel Cream *(Low carb version)*

Carb Count: < 2
Bucket glass, fill with ice.

1 oz Vodka
1/8 oz Cherry flavored sugar-free syrup
1/8 oz Caramel flavored sugar-free syrup
2 oz Atkins Advantage Vanilla Shake

Caramel Kiss *(Low carb version)*

Carb Count: < 2
Bucket glass, fill with ice.

1 oz Vodka
1/8 oz Cherry flavored sugar-free syrup
1/8 oz Caramel flavored sugar-free syrup
2 oz Atkins Advantage Chocolate Shake

Caramel Strawberries *(Low carb version)*

Carb Count: < 2.25
Bucket glass, fill with ice.

1 oz Vanilla Vodka
1/4 oz Butterscotch Schnapps
2 oz Atkins Advantage Strawberry Shake.

Fill the glass with sparkling water.

Caramel Berries *(Low carb version)*

Carb Count: < 2.25
Bucket glass, fill with ice.

1 oz Raspberry Rum
1/4 oz Butterscotch Schnapps
2 oz Atkins Advantage Strawberry Shake.

Fill the glass with sparkling water.

CC Coke *(Low carb version)*

Carb Count: < 1
Bucket glass, fill with ice.

1 oz ***Canadian Club*** Whiskey

Fill the glass with diet Coke.

Champagne Spritzer *(Low carb version)*

Carb Count: = 2
Champagne flute, chilled.

2 oz Dry Champagne (chilled)
2 oz Sparkling water (chilled)

For a touch more flavor, add a drop or two of peach or raspberry sugar free syrup. Watermelon and orange are also good. Mixing all four, (use just a drop of each one), gives the drink a fun tropical flavor. Please see the following note.

I do not recommend using sugar-free pineapple flavoring, for some reason the combination smells like cheap gasoline.

Champagne Berry Spritzer *(Low carb version)*

Carb Count: = 2
Champagne flute, chilled.

2 oz Dry Champagne (chilled)
2 oz Sparkling water (chilled)
1/8 oz Blackberry flavored sugar-free syrup
1/8 oz Strawberry flavored sugar-free syrup

Champagne Spritzer 2 *(Low carb version)*

Carb Count: < 1.5
Champagne flute, chilled.

1 oz Dry champagne (chilled)
2 oz White wine (chilled)
1 oz Sparkling water (chilled)

Cherry Rum and Coke *(Low carb version)*

Carb Count: < 1
Bucket glass, fill with ice.

1 oz Rum

Fill the glass with diet Cherry Coke or diet Dr. Pepper.

Cherry Spice Coke *(Low carb version)*

Carb Count: < 1
Bucket glass, fill with ice.

1 oz Vanilla Spice Rum

Fill the glass with diet cherry cola.

Cherry Whiskey *(Low carb version)*

Carb Count: < 1
Bucket glass, fill with ice.

1 oz Whiskey

Fill the glass with diet cherry soda or diet Cherry 7-Up.

Cherry Whiskey Coke *(Low carb version)*

Carb Count: < 1
Bucket glass, fill with ice.

1 oz Whiskey

Fill the glass with diet Cherry Coke or diet Dr. Pepper.

Chi-Chi *(Low carb version)*

Carb Count: < 3.5
In a blender combine:

1 cup Ice
1 oz Vodka
2 oz Low carb Pina Colada mix
1 oz Pineapple juice
1 oz Sparkling water

Blend and pour into a large specialty glass.

Budweiser History: Paving the way to destiny?

According to rumor, immediately after August III was born, and before he was allowed to nurse for the first time, his father (Eberhard Anheuser) gave him an eyedropper of Budweiser beer. I guess you would call that beer with a milk chaser!

Chocolate Cupcake *(Low carb version)*

Carb Count: < 1
Martini glass, chilled, no ice.
Shake and strain:

1 oz	***Absolut Citron*** Vodka
1/8 oz	Hazelnut flavored sugar-free syrup
Splash	Diet 7-Up or sparkling water
Splash	Lemon juice

Christmas Captain *(Low carb version)*

Carb Count: < 1
Bucket glass, fill with ice.

1 oz	***Captain Morgan's*** Rum
1/8 oz	Peppermint flavored sugar-free syrup

Fill the glass with diet Cherry Coke.

Coconut Cream *(Low carb version)*

Carb Count: < 1
Bucket glass, fill with ice.

1 oz	Coconut Rum

Fill the glass with diet cream soda.

Coconut Creamsickle *(Low carb version)*

Carb Count: < 1
Bucket glass, fill with ice.

1/2 oz	***Malibu*** Coconut Rum
1/2 oz	Vanilla Vodka

Fill the glass with diet orange soda.

Collins - Country *(Low carb version)*

Carb Count: < 1
Tall glass, fill with ice.

3/4 oz	***Absolut Kurrent*** Vodka
3/4 oz	***Absolut Mandarin*** Vodka
1 1/2 oz	Club soda
2 oz	Low carb sweet and sour

Collins - John *(Low carb version)*

Carb Count: < 1
Tall glass, fill with ice.

1 oz	Bourbon or whiskey
1 1/2 oz	Club soda
2 oz	Low carb sweet and sour

Collins - Pucker Up *(Low carb version)*

Carb Count: < 1
Tall glass, fill with ice.

1/2 oz	Vanilla Vodka
1/2 oz	Raspberry Vodka
1/2 oz	Lemon Vodka
1/2 oz	Lime Vodka
1 1/2 oz	Club soda
2 oz	Low carb sweet and sour

In 1959, Coors' started the first recycling program in the country. Offering 1 cent for each can returned.

Collins - Southern *(Low carb version)*

Carb Count: < 1
Tall glass, fill with ice.

1 oz	Vodka
1/4 oz	Peach flavored sugar-free syrup
1 1/2 oz	Club soda
2 oz	Low carb sweet and sour

Collins - Tom *(Low carb version)*

Carb Count: < 1
Tall glass, fill with ice.

1 oz	Gin
1 1/2 oz	Club soda
2 oz	Low carb sweet and sour

Collins - Vodka *(Low carb version)*

Carb Count: < 1
Tall glass, fill with ice.

1 oz	Vodka
1 1/2 oz	Club soda
2 oz	Low carb sweet and sour

Cosmopolitan *(Low carb version)*

Carb Count: < 2
Cocktail glass, chilled. Shake and strain:

1 oz	Vodka
1/4 oz	Vanilla Vodka
1/8 oz	Cherry flavored sugar-free syrup or Amaretto flavored sugar-free syrup
1/2 oz	Cranberry juice

Garnish with a lemon slice.

Crown and Coke *(Low carb version)*

Carb Count: < 1
Bucket glass, fill with ice.

1 oz ***Crown Royal*** Whiskey

Fill the glass with diet Coke.

Cuba Libre *(Low carb version)*

Carb Count: < 1
Bucket glass, fill with ice.

1 oz Rum

Fill the glass with diet Coke, or diet Lime Coke. Garnish with a lime slice.

Daiquiri *(Low carb version)*

Carb Count: < 1.5
In a blender combine:

1/3 cup	Ice
1 oz	***Bacardi*** Light Rum
2 oz	Low carb sweet and sour
Splash	Lemon juice
1 oz	Sparkling water or diet 7-Up

Blend until the drink is a smooth slush. Serve in a chilled cocktail or specialty glass.

> What are the top three reasons bartenders get fired? Theft, drinking on the job, and not showing up for work.

Daiquiri - Banana *(Low carb version)*

Carb Count: < 1.5
In a blender combine:

1/3 cup	Ice
1/2 oz	***Malibu*** Coconut Rum
1/2 oz	Banana Rum
1/8 oz	Banana flavored sugar-free syrup
1/8 oz	Coconut flavored sugar-free syrup
2 oz	Low carb sweet and sour
Splash	Lemon juice
1 oz	Sparkling water or diet 7-Up

Blend until the drink is a smooth slush. Serve in a chilled cocktail or specialty glass.

Daiquiri - Blackberry *(Low carb version)*

Carb Count: < 1.5
In a blender combine:

1/3 cup	Ice
1 oz	Raspberry Rum
1/8 oz	Blackberry flavored sugar-free syrup
1/8 oz	Raspberry flavored sugar-free syrup
2 oz	Low carb sweet and sour
Splash	Lemon juice
1 oz	Sparkling water or diet 7-Up

Blend until the drink is a smooth slush. Serve in a chilled cocktail or specialty glass.

Daiquiri - Peach *(Low carb version)*

Carb Count: < 1.5
In a blender combine:

1/3 cup	Ice
1 oz	***Bacardi*** Light Rum
1/4 oz	Peach flavored sugar-free syrup
2 oz	Low carb sweet and sour
Splash	Lemon juice
1 oz	Sparkling water or diet 7-Up

Blend until the drink is a smooth slush. Serve in a chilled cocktail or specialty glass.

Daiquiri - Strawberry *(Low carb version)*

Carb Count: < 1.5
In a blender combine:

1/3 cup	Ice
1 oz	Strawberry Rum
1/4 oz	Strawberry flavored sugar-free syrup
2 oz	Low carb sweet and sour
Splash	Lemon juice
1 oz	Sparkling water or diet 7-Up

Blend until the drink is a smooth slush. Serve in a chilled cocktail or specialty glass.

Danish Lover

Carb Count: < 5.75
Rocks glass, fill with ice.

1 oz	Aquavit (Caraway flavored vodka)
1/2 oz	***Kahlua***

Depth Charge/Boilermaker *(Low carb version)*

Carb Count: < 1.5
Pounder glass, chilled.

Half fill a pounder glass with a low carb beer. Serve with 1 oz of hard liquor (vodka, rum, gin, tequila or whiskey) in a shot glass. The customer drops the shot into the glass of beer.

Dragon Bite *(Low carb version)*

Carb Count: < 1
Rocks glass, fill with ice.

1-1/2 oz	Vodka
1/8 oz	Crème de Menthe sugar-free syrup, or Peppermint flavored sugar-free syrup
Splash	Sparkling water or diet 7-Up

Dreamy Creamsickle *(Low carb version)*

Carb Count: < 2
Bucket glass, fill with ice.
Shake and strain:

1 oz	Orange Rum
1/8 oz	Orange flavored sugar-free syrup

Fill the glass with Atkins Advantage Vanilla Shake.

Fizzy Navel *(Low carb version)*

Carb Count: < 3.25
Bucket glass, fill with ice.

1 oz	Vodka
1/8 oz	Peach flavored sugar-free syrup
1 oz	Orange juice

Fill the glass with Snapple diet peach tea.

Fog Cutter *(Low carb version)*

Carb Count: < 3.5
Tall glass, fill with ice.

1/8 oz	Brandy flavored sugar-free syrup
1/2 oz	Light Rum
1/2 oz	Gold Rum
1/2 oz	Gin
1-1/2 oz	Low carb sweet and sour
1 oz	Orange juice

French Bikini *(Low carb version)*

Carb Count: < 2
Bucket glass, fill with ice.

1-1/2 oz	Rum
1/8 oz	Chocolate flavored sugar-free syrup
1/8 oz	Rootbeer flavored sugar-free syrup
2 oz	Atkins Advantage Strawberry Supreme Shake

French Panties *(Low carb version)*

Carb Count: < 2
Bucket glass, fill with ice.

1-1/2 oz	Vodka
1/8 oz	Chocolate flavored sugar-free syrup
1/8 oz	Rootbeer flavored sugar-free syrup
2 oz	Atkins Advantage Strawberry Supreme Shake

Gimlet *(Low carb version)*

Carb Count: < 1
Rocks glass, fill with ice.

1-1/2 oz	Gin
1/2 oz	Low carb sweet and sour
Splash	Lime juice

Gin 'n Tonic *(Low carb version)*

Carb Count: < 1
Bucket glass, fill with ice.

1 oz Gin

Fill the glass with diet tonic water.

Around 1825, tonic water was invented. Tonic water was originally called *India Tonic Water*. It contains Quinine, and was developed to help prevent Malaria from striking the British soldiers fighting in the East Indian jungles.

The taste of Quinine is quite bitter. To get the soldiers to drink the tonic water, it was mixed with gin. This quickly became a popular combination.

Another problem was to get the men to eat citrus fruits to help fight scurvy, an illness common on long ship voyages, caused by a lack of vitamin C. Again, gin came to the rescue. Thus was born the "*gin and tonic with a twist of lime.*"

How popular was this new combination? Well, as Winston Churchill once said, "The gin and tonic has saved more Englishmen's lives, and minds, than all the doctors in the empire."

Ginger Snap *(Low carb version)*

Carb Count: < 1
Bucket glass, fill with ice.

1 oz Whiskey

Fill the glass with diet ginger ale.

Gin Rickey *(Low carb version)*

Carb Count: < 1
Bucket glass, fill with ice.

1 oz Gin

Fill the glass with sparkling water or club soda.

Godchild *(Low carb version)*

Carb Count: < 3.75
Rocks glass, fill with ice.

1-3/4 oz Brandy
1/4 oz Amaretto flavored sugar-free syrup

Fill the glass with sparkling water.

Godfather *(Low carb version)*

Carb Count: < 1
Rocks glass, fill with ice.

1-3/4 oz Scotch
1/4 oz Amaretto flavored sugar-free syrup

Fill the glass with sparkling water.

Godmother *(Low carb version)*

Carb Count: < 1
Rocks glass, fill with ice.

1-3/4 oz Vodka
1/4 oz Amaretto flavored sugar-free syrup

Fill the glass with sparkling water.

Grape Knee High *(Low carb version)*

Carb Count: < 1
Bucket glass, fill with ice.

1 oz Vodka
1/8 oz Grape flavored sugar-free syrup
1-1/2 oz Low carb sweet and sour

Fill the glass with sparkling water or diet 7-Up.

Grape Spice Coke *(Low carb version)*

Carb Count: < 1
Bucket glass, fill with ice.

1 oz Vanilla Spice Rum

Fill the glass with diet grape cola.

Greyhound *(Low carb version)*

Carb Count: < 4
Bucket glass, fill with ice.

1 oz Vodka
1 oz Grapefruit juice
1/2 oz Low carb sweet and sour

Greyhound Puppy *(Low carb version)*

Carb Count: < 1
Tall glass, fill with ice.

1 oz Vodka

Fill the glass with diet grapefruit soda or Crystal Light Ruby Red Grapefruit drink.

Harvey Wallbanger *(Low carb version)*

Carb Count: < 3.25
Bucket glass, fill with ice.

1 oz Vodka
1 oz Orange juice

Top with 1/8 oz French Vanilla flavored sugar-free syrup.

Hawaiian Breeze *(Low carb version)*

Carb Count: < 1.5
Champagne flute, chilled.

1 oz Dry champagne (chilled)
2 oz White wine (chilled)
1 oz Sparkling water (chilled)
1/2 tsp Strawberry flavored sugar-free syrup
1/2 tsp Coconut flavored sugar-free syrup
1/2 tsp Banana flavored sugar-free syrup

> Want to increase tips? SMILE more! Studies show that friendly bartenders make nearly twice the tips of their less enchanting coworkers.

Hawaiian Driver *(Low carb version)*

Carb Count: < 4.25
Bucket glass, fill with ice.

1 oz Vodka
1/2 oz Pineapple juice
1/2 oz Orange juice

Fill the glass with sparkling water, club soda, or diet 7-Up.

Hazelnut Cream Dream *(Low carb version)*

Carb Count: < 2
Bucket glass, fill with ice.
Shake and strain:

1 oz Vodka
1/8 oz Hazelnut flavored sugar-free syrup

Fill the glass with Atkins Advantage Vanilla Shake.

Highball *(Low carb version)*

Carb Count: < 1
Bucket glass, fill with ice.

1 oz Bourbon

Fill the glass with diet ginger ale.

Holy Bananas! *(Low carb version)*

Carb Count: < 4.15
Brandy snifter, warmed.

1/4 oz ***99 Bananas***
1 oz ***Christian Brothers*** Brandy

Honey Dew *(Low carb version)*

Carb Count: < 1.5
Tall glass, fill with ice.

1 oz	Vodka
1/8 oz	Watermelon flavored sugar-free syrup

Add 2 oz chilled white wine, or 1 oz chilled dry champagne. Fill the glass with Crystal Light Pink Lemonade.

Hot Vodka Toddy *(Low carb version)*

Carb Count: < 1
Large coffee cup, warmed.

1 oz	Orange or Lemon Vodka

Fill the cup with hot water. A tea bag may be added. Serve with Equal or Sweet and Low, and a lemon slice.

Hot Whiskey Toddy *(Low carb version)*

Carb Count: < 1
Large coffee cup, warmed.

1 oz	Whiskey

Fill the cup with hot water. A tea bag may be added. Serve with Equal or Sweet and Low, and a lemon slice.

Hurricane *(Low carb version)*

Carb Count: < 3.5
Tall glass, fill with ice.

1 oz	Gold Rum
1 oz	Light Rum
2 oz	Low carb sweet and sour
1 oz	Orange juice
Splash	Lime juice

Top with 1/8 oz cherry flavored sugar-free syrup.

Hypnotic Daze *(Low carb version)*

Carb Count: < 2
Bucket glass, fill with ice.
Shake and strain:

1 oz	Vodka
1/2 oz	***Malibu*** Coconut Rum
1/4 oz	Pineapple juice
1/8 oz	Orange flavored sugar-free syrup
2 drops	Blue food coloring

Irish Ambush *(Low carb version)*

Carb Count: < 1
Martini glass, chilled, no ice.
Shake and strain:

1-1/2 oz	Irish Whiskey
1/8 oz	Cherry flavored sugar-free syrup
Splash	Sparkling water or club soda

Jagar Bomb *(Low carb version)*

Carb Count: < 11.25
Tall glass, no ice.

1 oz ***Jagermeister*** (served in a shot glass)

Fill the glass 3/4 full with diet Mt. Dew.

Jolly Ranchers - Grape *(Low carb version)*

Carb Count: < 1
Tall glass, fill with ice.

1 oz	Vodka
1 oz	Grape flavored sugar-free syrup

Fill the glass with an even mix of diet 7-Up and sparkling water or club soda. Garnish with a cherry.

Jolly Ranchers - Peach *(Low carb version)*

Carb Count: < 1
Tall glass, fill with ice.

1 oz Vodka
1 oz Peach flavored sugar-free syrup

Fill the glass with an even mix of diet 7-Up and sparkling water or club soda. Garnish with a cherry.

Jolly Ranchers - Sour Apple *(Low carb version)*

Carb Count: < 1
Tall glass, fill with ice.

1 oz Vodka
1 oz Sour Apple flavored sugar-free syrup

Fill the glass with an even mix of diet 7-Up and sparkling water or club soda. Garnish with a cherry.

Jolly Ranchers - Watermelon *(Low carb version)*

Carb Count: < 1
Tall glass, fill with ice.

1 oz Vodka
1 oz Watermelon flavored sugar-free syrup

Fill the glass with an even mix of diet 7-Up and sparkling water or club soda. Garnish with a cherry.

Kamikaze *(Low carb version)*

Carb Count: < 1
Rocks glass, fill with ice.

1 oz ***Smirnoff Lime Twist*** Vodka
1/8 oz Orange flavored sugar-free syrup
1/8 oz Lime juice
1 oz Low carb sweet and sour

Lemon Drop (mixed drink) ***(Low carb version)***

Carb Count: < 2
Rocks glass, fill with ice.

1-1/2 oz	Lemon Vodka
1/8 oz	Orange flavored sugar-free syrup
1/4 oz	Fresh lemon juice

Fill the glass with Low carb sweet and sour. Garnish with a lemon slice.

Lemon Meringue ***(Low carb version)***

Carb Count: < 1
Bucket glass, fill with ice.

1/2 oz	Vanilla Vodka
1/2 oz	Lemon Vodka
Splash	Lemon juice

Fill the glass with diet cream soda.

Lemon Rita ***(Low carb version)***

Carb Count: < 1
Bucket glass, fill with ice.

1 oz	Citrus Rum
Splash	Lemon juice

Fill the glass with diet lemon-lime soda or diet 7-Up.

Lemon Rum and Pepsi ***(Low carb version)***

Carb Count: < 1
Bucket glass, fill with ice.

1 oz	Rum

Fill the glass with diet Lemon Pepsi Twist or diet Lemon Coke.

Lemon Whiskey Twister *(Low carb version)*

Carb Count: < 1
Bucket glass, fill with ice.

1 oz	Whiskey
Splash	Lemon juice

Fill the glass with diet 7-Up.

Lemon Whiskey and Pepsi *(Low carb version)*

Carb Count: < 1
Bucket glass, fill with ice.

1 oz Whiskey

Fill the glass with diet Lemon Pepsi Twist.

Lime Willy *(Low carb version)*

Carb Count: < 1
Bucket glass, fill with ice.

1 oz	Rum
Splash	Lime juice

Fill the glass with diet 7-Up. Garnish with a lime slice.

Little Wall Banger *(Low carb version)*

Carb Count: < 1
Tall glass, fill with ice.

1 oz Vodka

Nearly fill the glass with diet orange soda, top with 1/8 oz French Vanilla flavored sugar-free syrup.

Little Screwdriver *(Low carb version)*

Carb Count: < 1
Tall glass, fill with ice.

1 oz Vodka or orange vodka

Fill the glass with diet orange soda.

Madras *(Low carb version)*

Carb Count: < 3.5
Bucket glass, fill with ice.

1 oz Vodka
1/2 oz Orange juice
1/2 oz Cranberry juice

Fill the glass sparkling water, club soda, diet orange soda or diet 7-Up.

Malibu Coke *(Low carb version)*

Carb Count: < 1
Bucket glass, fill with ice.

1 oz ***Malibu*** Coconut Rum

Fill the glass with diet Coke or diet Lemon Coke.

Mai-Tai *(Low carb version)*

Carb Count: < 4
Tall glass, fill with ice.

1 oz Light Rum or Cherry Rum
1/2 oz Pineapple juice
2 oz Low carb sweet and sour
1/8 oz Cherry flavored sugar-free syrup

Nearly fill the glass with sparkling water. Float 1/2 oz ***Myers'*** rum on top.

Midori Sour *(Low carb version)*

Carb Count: < 4

Bucket glass, fill with ice.

1/4 oz ***Midori***

Fill the glass with Low carb sweet and sour or Crystal Light lemonade.

Mimosa *(Low carb version)*

Carb Count: < 4

Tall glass, fill with ice.

3 oz Blush or white wine (chilled)
1 oz Orange juice (chilled)
2 oz Sparkling water

Mint Julep *(Low carb version)*

Carb Count: < 1

The Mint Julep has been a popular drink of the Deep South for over 200 years. MGM/UA and Sean Connery made it famous in the 1964 movie, ***Goldfinger.***

Bucket glass, 1/2 fill with ice.

2 oz Bourbon
5 or 6 Fresh mint leaves
1/2 oz Diet 7-Up

Muddle (mash) the ice, mint leaves, diet 7-Up and half the bourbon together. Next, add the rest of the bourbon and fill the glass with ice. Garnish with fresh mint leaves.

Mojito *(Low carb version)*

Carb Count: < 2.25

This famous drink is from the 2002 MGM/UA movie, ***Die Another Day***, starring Pierce Brosnan.

Bucket glass, fill with ice.

1 oz	Light Rum
1/8 tsp.	Sugar substitute (to taste)

Squeeze the juice from half a lime into the drink then fill the glass with soda water. Garnish with Mojito mint sprigs.

Morning Mimosa *(Low carb version)*

Carb Count: < 3.75

Champagne glass, chilled. Shake and strain:

1 oz	Vodka
1/8 oz	Orange flavored sugar-free syrup
2 oz	White wine (chilled)
1 oz	Orange juice (chilled)

Old Fashioned *(Low carb version)*

Carb Count: < 1

Bucket glass, fill with ice.

2 Dashes	Bitters
1/8 oz	Orange flavored sugar-free syrup
1/8 oz	Cherry flavored sugar-free syrup
1 oz	***Jim Beam*** Bourbon

Fill the glass with club soda.

Orange Coconuts *(Low carb version)*

Carb Count: < 1
Bucket glass, fill with ice.

1 oz ***Malibu*** Coconut Rum

Fill the glass with diet orange soda.

Panty Dropper *(Low carb version)*

Carb Count: < 5.75
Bucket glass, fill with ice.

1/4 oz ***Kahlua***
1/4 oz Sloe Gin
3/4 oz Vodka

Fill the glass with diet cream soda.

Panty Raid *(Low carb version)*

Carb Count: < 5.25
Bucket glass, fill with ice.

1/2 oz Pear Brandy
1/4 oz ***Wild Spirit***
3/4 oz Vanilla Vodka

Fill the glass with diet cream soda.

Panty Snapper *(Low carb version)*

Carb Count: < 5.75
Bucket glass, fill with ice.

1/4 oz ***Kahlua***
1/4 oz ***Wild Spirit***
3/4 oz Vanilla Vodka

Fill the glass with diet cream soda.

Pass the Buck *(Low carb version)*

Carb Count: < 2
Bucket glass, fill with ice.

1 oz Vodka
1/8 oz Chocolate flavored sugar-free syrup
1/8 oz Rootbeer flavored sugar-free syrup
2 oz Atkins Advantage Chocolate Shake

Peaches 'n Cream Dream *(Low carb version)*

Carb Count: < 2
Bucket glass, fill with ice.
Shake and strain:

1 oz Vodka
1/8 oz Peach flavored sugar-free syrup

Fill the glass with Atkins Advantage Vanilla Shake.

Peach Flame *(Low carb version)*

Carb Count: < 4.75
Brandy snifter, warmed.

1/4 oz Peach Schnapps
1 oz ***Christian Brothers*** Brandy

Peachy Keen *(Low carb version)*

Carb Count: < 2.25
Bucket glass, fill with ice.

1 oz Raspberry Rum
1/4 oz Peach Schnapps
2 oz Atkins Advantage Strawberry Supreme Shake.

Fill the glass with sparkling water.

Pina Colada *(Low carb version)*

Carb Count: < 7

In a blender add:

- 1 cup Ice
- 1 oz Light Rum (or ***Malibu***)
- 3 oz Low Carb Pina Colada mix
- 1 oz Pineapple juice

Blend and pour into a large cocktail glass. Garnish with a cherry.

Pina Colada 2 *(Low carb version)*

Carb Count: < 4

In a blender add:

- 1 cup Ice
- 1 oz Light Rum (or ***Malibu***)
- 3 oz Low carb Pina Colada mix
- 1/2 oz Sparkling water

Blend and pour into a large cocktail glass. Garnish with a cherry.

A Little Bacardi History

While working a lot of lonely nights perfecting his rum recipes, Don Bacardi befriended a family of fruit bats who were living in the distillery rafters.

Apparently this friendship blossomed to become quite an ongoing relationship. Don Bacardi later designed the famous Bacardi logo, a large black bat, in remembrance of his furry friends.

Pineapple Boo/Pine Boo *(Low carb version)*

Carb Count: < 4.5
Bucket glass, fill with ice.

1 oz ***Malibu*** Coconut Rum
1 oz Pineapple juice

Fill the glass with sparkling water or diet 7-Up.

Pineapple Upside Down Cake *(Low carb version)*

Carb Count: < 2.75
Shot glass, chilled, no ice.
Shake and strain:

1/2 oz Pineapple juice
1/2 oz ***Stoli*** Vanilla Vodka
1/8 oz Cherry flavored sugar-free syrup
1 splash Diet 7-Up or sparkling water

Pink Russian *(Low carb version)*

Carb Count: < 4.75
Rocks glass, fill with ice.

1 oz Vanilla Vodka
1/4 oz ***Tequila Rose*** Strawberry Tequila
1/4 oz ***Kahlua***

Pink Russian #2 *(Low carb version)*

Carb Count: < 2.25
Bucket glass, fill with ice.

1 oz Vanilla Vodka
1/4 oz ***Tequila Rose*** Strawberry Tequila

Fill the glass with Atkins Advantage Chocolate Shake.

Poppers/Slammers *(Low carb version)*

Carb Count: < 1
Rocks glass, no ice.

1 oz	Any hard liquor (whiskey, gin, vodka, rum or tequila)
Splash	Diet 7-Up, sparkling water or club soda

The customer covers the glass with his hand, slams it on the counter, and drinks the shot.

I suggest customers place one hand face up on the counter, and slam the covered glass into his open palm. This helps prevent people getting too wild and breaking the glass.

Presbyterian/Press *(Low carb version)*

Carb Count: < 1
Bucket glass, fill with ice.

1 oz Bourbon

Fill the glass with equal parts of diet ginger ale and sparkling water or club soda.

Before trucks were invented to deliver the beer, the Anheuser-Busch Brewing Company used horse drawn delivery wagons.

A Dalmatian dog always rode with the team. His duty was to protect the valuable horses and cargo from theft, while the driver was making his deliveries. If you look closely, you will see a Dalmatian riding in the wagon or sleigh, anytime the Budweiser Clydesdales are performing.

Purple Hooter *(Low carb version)*

Carb Count: < 1
Martini glass, chilled, no ice.
Shake and strain:

1 oz	Vodka
1/8 oz	Grape flavored sugar- free syrup
1/2 oz	Low carb sweet and sour

Purple Hooter #2 *(Low carb version)*

Carb Count: < 3
Martini glass, chilled, no ice.
Shake and strain:

1 oz	Vodka
1/4 oz	***Chambord***
1/2 oz	Low carb sweet and sour

Raspberry Cream *(Low carb version)*

Carb Count: < 1
Bucket glass, fill with ice.

3/4 oz	Raspberry Vodka
1/4 oz	Vanilla Vodka

Fill the glass with diet cream soda or Crystal Light Raspberry Ice drink mix.

Did you know……

Besides the famous Bacardi rums, Bacardi Ltd, also owns Dewar's scotch, Bombay Sapphire gin, and has just agreed to buy the Grey Goose vodka company. Grey Goose is currently the best selling vodka in the United States.

Red Beer *(Low carb version)*

Carb Count: < 6.75 (light beer)
Carb Count: < 4.50 (ultra light beer)
Pounder glass, chilled, no ice.

14 oz	Low Carb Beer (use light beer if low carb is not available)
1 oz	Tomato juice

Pour the beer first, then add the tomato juice. If you put the tomato juice in first, the beer will foam all over the place and make a mess.

Red Snapper *(Low carb version)*

Carb Count: < 2
In a mixing glass, 1/3 filled with ice, combine:

1 oz	Gin
2-3 dashes	Salt and pepper
2 dashes	Wocerstershire Sauce
2 dashes	Red Tabasco
2 dashes	Green Tabasco *(*** HOT***)*
1 oz	Tomato juice
Splash	Lime juice

Shake thoroughly, then strain into a bucket glass filled with ice. The rim may be salted if desired.

Rooty Tooty *(Low carb version)*

Carb Count: < 2
Bucket glass, fill with ice.
Shake and strain:

1 oz	Vanilla Vodka
1/4 oz	Rootbeer flavored sugar-free syrup

Fill the glass with Atkins Advantage Strawberry Supreme Shake.

Rum and Coke *(Low carb version)*

Carb Count: < 1
Bucket glass, fill with ice.

1 oz Rum

Fill the glass with diet Coke.

Rum and 7 *(Low carb version)*

Carb Count: < 1
Bucket glass, fill with ice.

1 oz Rum

Fill the glass with diet 7-Up.

Rum Runner *(Low carb version)*

Carb Count: < 4.5
Tall glass, fill with ice.

1/2 oz	Light Rum
1 oz	Gold Rum
1/8 oz	Blackberry flavored sugar-free syrup
1/8 oz	Brandy flavored sugar-free syrup
1/8 oz	Banana flavored sugar-free syrup
1-1/2 oz	Low carb sweet and sour
1 oz	Orange juice

Nearly fill the glass with diet orange soda. Top with 1/8 oz cherry flavored sugar-free syrup.

> Sloe Gin has no gin in it! Is a sweet liqueur made from Sloeberries - a wild berry similar to a raspberry.

Rum Runner – Caribbean *(Low carb version)*

Carb Count: < 2
Make with ***Cabana Boy*** rums.
Hurricane glass, fill with ice.

1/2 oz	Pineapple-Coconut Rum
1/2 oz	Strawberry - Kiwi Rum
1/2 oz	Coconut Rum
1/2 oz	Banana Rum
1-1/2 oz	Low carb sweet and sour

Nearly fill the glass with diet orange soda. Top with 1/8 oz cherry flavored sugar-free syrup.

Rum Runner - San Francisco *(Low carb version)*

Carb Count: < 2
Tall glass, fill with ice.

1/3 oz	Light Rum
1/3 oz	Gold Rum
1/3 oz	151 Rum
1/3 oz	Coconut Rum
1-1/2 oz	Low carb sweet and sour
1/8 oz	Watermelon flavored sugar-free syrup.

Nearly fill the glass with diet orange soda. Top with 1/8 oz grape or raspberry flavored sugar-free syrup.

> Love a cold Bloody Mary, but hate the watered down taste when the ice melts? Try freezing cherry tomatoes, and using them in place of the ice cubes. For best results, stick picks into the tomatoes BEFORE freezing.

Rum Runner - Tropical Dreams *(Low carb version)*

Carb Count: < 2
Make with ***Cabana Boy*** rums.
Hurricane glass, fill with ice.

1/2 oz	Pineapple-Coconut Rum
1/2 oz	Banana Rum
1/2 oz	Raspberry Rum
1/2 oz	Coconut Rum
1-1/2 oz	Low carb sweet and sour
1/8 oz	Raspberry flavored sugar-free syrup.

Nearly fill the glass with diet orange soda. Top with 1/8 oz cherry flavored sugar-free syrup.

Rum Runner - Very Berry *(Low carb version)*

Carb Count: < 2
Make with ***Cabana Boy*** rums.
Hurricane glass, fill with ice.

1/2 oz	Strawberry - Kiwi Rum
1/2 oz	Strawberry - Banana Rum
1/2 oz	Coconut Rum
1-1/2 oz	Low carb sweet and sour

Nearly fill the glass with diet orange soda. Top with 1/8 oz raspberry or blackberry flavored sugar-free syrup.

Salty Dog *(Low carb version)*

Carb Count: < 3.5
Bucket glass, salt rim, fill with ice.

1 oz	Vodka
1 oz	Grapefruit juice

Salty Puppy *(Low carb version)*

Carb Count: < 1
Tall glass, salt rim, fill with ice.

1 oz Vodka

Fill the glass with diet grapefruit soda or Crystal Light Ruby Red Grapefruit drink.

Sangria *(Low carb version)*

Carb Count: < 9
Tall glass, fill with ice.

4 oz	Red table wine (dry)
1 oz	Orange juice
1/8 oz	Cherry flavored sugar-free syrup
1/8 oz	Peach flavored sugar-free syrup
1/2 oz	Orange vodka
1/4 oz	Lime juice
1-1/2 oz	Low carb sweet and sour

Scooby Snacks *(Low carb version)*

Carb Count: < 4
Bucket glass, fill with ice

1 oz	***Malibu*** Rum
1/4 oz	***Midori***
2 oz	Atkins Advantage Vanilla Shake

> Morning sickness? Flu? Hangover? Try a full glass of club soda (no ice), and a couple drops of Bitters. Simple and effective!

Scooby Snacks #2 *(Low carb version)*

Carb Count: < 2
Bucket glass, fill with ice

1 oz	***Malibu*** Rum
1/8 oz	Watermelon flavored sugar-free syrup
2 oz	Atkins Advantage Strawberry Supreme Shake

Scorpion Sting *(Low carb version)*

Carb Count: < 5.75
Tall glass, fill with ice.

3/4 oz	Vodka
3/4 oz	Rum
1/2 oz	Gin
1/8 oz	Brandy flavored sugar-free syrup
1/8 oz	Orange flavored sugar-free syrup
1/4 oz	Lime juice
1 oz	Orange juice
1-1/2 oz	Low carb sweet and sour

Scotch and Soda

Carb Count: < 1
Bucket glass, fill with ice.

1 oz Scotch

Fill the glass with club soda.

Screaming Pink Lemonade *(Low carb version)*

Carb Count: < 1
Tall glass, fill with ice.

1 oz Vodka

Fill the glass with Crystal Light Pink Grapefruit drink.

Screwdriver *(Low carb version)*

Carb Count: < 3.25
Bucket glass, fill with ice.

1 oz Vodka
1 oz Orange juice

Sea Breeze *(Low carb version)*

Carb Count: < 3.75
Bucket glass, fill with ice.

1 oz Vodka
1/2 oz Grapefruit juice
1/2 oz Cranberry juice

Fill the glass with sparkling water, diet 7-Up or diet grapefruit soda.

A Little Gin History

In 1820, James Burroughs, a pharmacist, developed what was to become one of the leading English gins. He built his distillery near the Thames River and the Tower of London. He had developed the recipe for his gin, but did not yet have a trademark name for his fine liquor. One day, deep in thought, he took a walk along the road to the Queen's palace. While watching the changing of the guards, he noted the exceptionally strong and fierce Yeomen (soldiers) guarding the Royal Palace, and inquired about them. A local merchant told him that the Yeomen were so tough because they ate a full ration of beef every day, so much meat that they were called "beef-eaters." Today, the symbol of the Yeoman graces each and every ***Beefeater Gin*** bottle.

7 and 7 *(7/7)* ***(Low carb version)***

Carb Count: < 1
Bucket glass, fill with ice.

1 oz ***Seagram's*** *7* Whisky

Fill the glass with diet 7-Up.

Sex on the Beach ***(Low carb version)***

Carb Count: < 4.50
Bucket glass, fill with ice.

1-1/2 oz Vodka
1/8 oz Peach flavored sugar-free syrup
1/2 oz Orange juice
1/2 oz Cranberry juice
1 oz Low carb sweet and sour

Fill the glass with sparkling water or diet 7-Up.

Sex on the Beach with a Georgia Peach

(Low carb version)

Carb Count: < 4.50
Tall glass, fill with ice.

1 oz ***Stoli*** Vanilla Vodka
1/8 oz Peach flavored sugar-free syrup
1/8 oz Raspberry flavored sugar-free syrup
1/2 oz Orange juice
1/2 oz Cranberry juice
1 oz Low carb sweet and sour

Fill the glass with sparkling water or diet 7-Up.

Skip and go Naked *(Low carb version)*

Carb Count: < 2.60 (light beer)
Carb Count: < 2.00 (ultra light beer)
Tall glass, fill with ice.

1 oz	Gin
2 oz	Low carb sweet and sour

Fill the glass with low carb beer (about 4 oz). Use light beer if low carb is not available.

Snow Shoe *(Low carb version)*

Carb Count: < 1
Rocks glass, fill with ice.

1-1/2 oz	***Wild Turkey*** Bourbon
1/8 oz	Crème de Menthe or peppermint flavored sugar-free syrup
Splash	Diet 7-Up

SoCo Stone Sour *(Low carb version)*

Carb Count: < 2
Bucket glass, fill with ice.

1/2 oz	***Southern Comfort***
Splash	Orange juice (chilled)

Fill the glass with Low carb sweet and sour or Crystal Light Lemonade.

> Once upon a time… in the Old West, in many towns prostitution was illegal. The bartenders figured out a way to keep the local economy running however – a shot of whiskey cost a small fortune, but with is came a girl's "attentions," which were free.

Sparkling Cherry Rum *(Low carb version)*

Carb Count: < 1
Bucket glass, fill with ice.

1 oz Rum

Fill the glass with diet cherry soda or diet Cherry 7-Up.

Strawberry Creamsickle *(Low carb version)*

Carb Count: < 1
Bucket glass, fill with ice.

1 oz Strawberry-Kiwi Rum

Fill the glass with Crystal Light Strawberry-Kiwi or Strawberry-Orange-Banana drink.

Surfer on Acid *(Low carb version)*

Carb Count: < 2.25
Rocks glass, fill with ice

1/8 oz Chocolate flavored sugar-free syrup
1/8 oz Rootbeer flavored sugar-free syrup
1 oz ***Malibu*** Coconut Rum
1/3 oz Pineapple juice

T & A Tease *(Low carb version)*

Carb Count: < 2.75
Make with ***Cabana Boy*** rum.
Bucket glass, fill with ice.

1 oz Pineapple-Coconut Rum
1/2 oz Pineapple juice

Fill the glass with diet strawberry-kiwi soda.

Teeny Bikini *(Low carb version)*

Carb Count: < 2
Bucket glass, fill with ice.

1-1/2 oz	Rum
1/8 oz	Watermelon flavored sugar-free syrup
1/8 oz	Rootbeer flavored sugar-free syrup
2 oz	Atkins Advantage Strawberry Supreme Shake

Tequila Driver *(Low carb version)*

Carb Count: < 3.25
Bucket glass, fill with ice.

1 oz	Tequila
1 oz	Orange juice

Fill the glass with sparkling water, diet orange soda, or Crystal Light Orange-Pineapple drink.

Tequila Sunrise *(Low carb version)*

Carb Count: < 3.25
Bucket glass, fill with ice.

1 oz	Tequila
1 oz	Orange juice

Nearly fill the glass with diet orange soda. Top with 1/8 oz cherry flavored sugar-free syrup.

> Hiccups? Try several drops of Bitters on a lime wedge. A few bites and the hiccups are gone! Simple and effective!

Tequila Sunset *(Low carb version)*

Carb Count: < 3.25
Bucket glass.

1/8 oz Blackberry flavored sugar-free syrup
(On the bottom, then fill the glass with ice.)
1 oz Tequila
1 oz Orange juice

Fill the glass with diet orange soda.

Tropical Wet Dream *(Low carb version)*

Carb Count: < 1
Make with ***Cabana Boy*** rum.
Bucket glass, fill with ice.

1/2 oz Strawberry-Banana Rum
1/2 oz Coconut Rum

Fill the glass with diet orange or diet strawberry soda or similar drink.

Tropical Tease *(Low carb version)*

Carb Count: < 1
Bucket glass, fill with ice.

1 oz ***Cabana Boy*** Strawberry-Banana Rum

Fill the glass with diet strawberry-kiwi soda.

> Is the splash drain for your beer taps smelling funky? Try pouring hot water down the drain, followed by a full glass of club soda.

Tsunami (*Low carb version)*

Carb Count: < 5.00
Tall glass, fill with ice.

1 oz	Vodka
1/8 oz	Peach flavored sugar-free syrup
1/8 oz	Strawberry flavored sugar-free syrup
1/8 oz	***Midori***
1/2 oz	Orange juice
1/2 oz	Cranberry juice
1 oz	Low carb sweet and sour

Fill the glass with sparkling water or diet 7-Up.

Twisted Bikini *(Low carb version)*

Carb Count: < 1
Pounder glass, fill with ice.

1-1/2 oz	Rum
1/8 oz	Chocolate flavored sugar-free syrup
1/8 oz	Rootbeer flavored sugar-free syrup

Fill the glass with diet Mt. Dew.

Twisted Pepsi Splash *(Low carb version)*

Carb Count: < 1
Bucket glass, fill with ice.

1/2 oz	Lime Vodka
1/2 oz	Lemon Vodka

Fill the glass with diet Pepsi Twist.

Toxic Waste *(Low carb version)*

Carb Count: < 2
Tall glass, fill with ice.

1/4 oz Orange Vodka
3/4 oz Rum
1/2 oz Tequila
1/8 oz Cherry flavored sugar-free syrup
1/8 oz Orange flavored sugar-free syrup
1/2 oz Grapefruit juice

Nearly fill the glass with diet coke. Top with 1/2 oz 151 rum.

Vanilla Berry Blitz *(Low carb version)*

Carb Count: < 2
Bucket glass, fill with ice.
Shake and strain:

1 oz Raspberry Vodka

Fill the glass with Atkins Advantage Vanilla Shake.

Vanilla Berry Boost *(Low carb version)*

Carb Count: < 2
Bucket glass, fill with ice.
Shake and strain:

1 oz Raspberry Rum

Fill the glass with Atkins Advantage Vanilla Shake.

Vanilla Rum and Coke *(Low carb version)*

Carb Count: < 1
Bucket glass, fill with ice.

1 oz Rum

Fill the glass with diet Vanilla Coke.

Velvet Coke *(Low carb version)*

Carb Count: < 1
Bucket glass, fill with ice.

1 oz ***Black Velvet*** Canadian Whiskey

Fill the glass with diet Coke.

Very Berry Coke *(Low carb version)*

Carb Count: < 1
Bucket glass, fill with ice.

1 oz Raspberry Vodka

Fill the glass with diet Cherry Coke.

Very Berry Seven *(Low carb version)*

Carb Count: < 1
Bucket glass, fill with ice.

3/4 oz Raspberry Rum
3/4 oz Strawberry Rum

Fill the glass with diet 7-Up.

Very Cherry Coke and Cream *(Low carb version)*

Carb Count: < 1
Bucket glass, fill with ice.

3/4 oz Raspberry Vodka
1/4 oz Vanilla Vodka

Fill the glass with equal parts of diet Cherry and diet Vanilla Coke.

Very Vanilla Coke *(Low carb version)*

Carb Count: < 1
Bucket glass, fill with ice.

1 oz Vanilla Vodka

Fill the glass with diet Vanilla Coke.

Vodka 'n Coke *(Low carb version)*

Carb Count: < 1
Bucket glass, fill with ice.

1 oz Vodka

Fill the glass with diet Coke.

Vodka 'n 7 *(Low carb version)*

Carb Count: < 1
Bucket glass, fill with ice.

1 oz Vodka

Fill the glass with diet 7-Up.

Vodka and Soda *(Low carb version)*

Carb Count: < 1
Bucket glass, fill with ice.

1 oz Vodka

Fill the glass with club soda.

Vodka 'n Tonic *(Low carb version)*

Carb Count: < 1
Bucket glass, fill with ice.

1 oz Vodka

Fill the glass with diet tonic water.

Vodka-Cranberry *(Low carb version)*

Carb Count: < 3.75
Bucket glass, fill with ice.

1 oz Vodka
1 oz Cranberry juice

Fill the glass with sparkling water, club soda, or diet 7-Up.

Vodka Creamsickle *(Low carb version)*

Carb Count: < 3.50
Bucket glass, fill with ice.

1 oz ***Stoli*** Vanilla Vodka
1 oz Orange juice

Fill the glass with sparkling water.

Vodka Key Lime *(Low carb version)*

Carb Count: < 2
Bucket glass, fill with ice.

1 oz ***Smirnoff Lime Twist*** Vodka
1/2 oz ***Stoli*** Vanilla Vodka

Fill the glass with Low carb sweet and sour.

Vodka Key Lime Pie *(Low carb version)*

Carb Count: < 2.50
Tall glass, fill with ice.

1 oz ***Smirnoff Lime Twist*** Vodka
1/2 oz ***Stoli*** Vanilla Vodka
1/8 oz Butterscotch flavored sugar-free syrup

Fill the glass with Low carb sweet and sour.

Vodka Lemon Meringue *(Low carb version)*

Carb Count: < 2.50
Tall glass, fill with ice.

1/2 oz ***Absolut Citron*** Vodka
1/2 oz ***Absolut*** Vanilla Vodka

Fill the glass with Low carb sweet and sour.

Vodka Lemon Meringue Pie *(Low carb version)*

Carb Count: < 2.50
Tall glass, fill with ice.

1/2 oz ***Absolut Citron*** Vodka
1/4 oz ***Absolut*** Vanilla Vodka
1/8 oz Butterscotch or caramel flavored sugar-free syrup

Fill the glass with Low carb sweet and sour

Vodka Press *(Low carb version)*

Carb Count: < 1
Bucket glass, fill with ice.

1 oz Vodka

Fill the glass with equal parts of diet ginger ale and sparkling water or club soda.

Washington Apple *(Low carb version)*

Carb Count: < 2
Shot glass, no ice.

1 oz ***Crown Royal*** Whiskey
1/8 oz Sour Apple flavored sugar-free syrup
1/2 oz Cranberry juice

Whiskey Coke *(Low carb version)*

Carb Count: < 1
Bucket glass, fill with ice.

1 oz Whiskey

Fill the glass with diet Coke.

Whiskey 'n Water

Carb Count: < 1
Bucket glass, fill with ice.

1 oz Whiskey

Fill the glass with water.

Whiskey Seven *(Low carb version)*

Carb Count: < 1
Bucket glass, fill with ice.

1 oz Whiskey

Fill the glass with diet 7-Up.

Whiskey Sour *(Low carb version)*

Carb Count: < 1
Bucket glass, fill with ice.

1 oz Whiskey

Fill the glass with Low carb sweet and sour.

> When cutting a customer off, make sure they get home safely. Offer to call a spouse, friend, or a cab. Document what steps you took. This will help to protect you and your bar.

Zipper *(Low carb version)*

Carb Count: < 4.50
Tall glass, fill with ice.

1/3 oz	Vanilla Rum
1/3 oz	Coconut Rum
1/3 oz	Light Rum
1/4 oz	Raspberry Vodka
1/8 oz	Banana flavored sugar-free syrup
1 oz	Orange juice
1-1/2 oz	Low carb sweet and sour

Nearly fill the glass with diet orange soda. Top with 1/8 oz grape or raspberry flavored sugar-free syrup.

Zombie *(Low carb version)*

Carb Count: < 4.50
Tall glass, fill with ice.

1 oz	Light Rum
1/2 oz	***Cabana Boy*** Wild Cherry Rum
1/8 oz	Orange flavored sugar-free syrup
1/8 oz	Cherry flavored sugar-free syrup
1 oz	Orange juice

Nearly fill the glass with Low carb sweet and sour. Top with 1/2 oz ***Bacardi*** 151 rum. Garnish with a cherry.

Sources for the 007 drinks:

"Drink Like 007," *M16 – The Home of 007*, 26th November 2002, <http://www.mi6.co.uk/sections/ articles/drink_like_007.php3?t=&s=articles>, (5 May 2004). **If you are a James Bond fan, you absolutely must see this site.**

"Make Mine a 007 – The James Bond Films," *The Minister of Martinis*, 2002, <http://home.earthlink.net/~atomic_rom/007/films.htm>, (5 May 2004).

"Why did James Bond want his martinis shaken, not stirred?," *The Straight Dope*, 28-Nov-2000, <http://www.straightdope.com/mailbag/mmartini.html>, (5 May 2004).

That's not a worm in your tequila, it is a butterfly caterpillar! This tasty treat is best served with lime wedges and salt. And don't forget to share. These caterpillars are considered an aphrodisiac in many countries!

Lemonades and Iced Teas

If you don't have Low carb sweet and sour, try using Crystal Light Lemonade or Crystal Light Pink Lemonade. They both work very well, and are available at almost every grocery or convenience store.

Black Opal *(Low carb version)*

Carb Count: < 2.50
Tall glass, fill with ice.

1/2 oz Vodka
1/2 oz Rum
1/2 oz Gin
1/8 oz Orange flavored sugar-free syrup
2 oz Low carb sweet and sour

Nearly fill the glass with diet 7-Up. Top with 1/4 oz ***Chambord.***

Black Opal #2 *(Low carb version)*

Carb Count: < 2
Tall glass, fill with ice.

1/2 oz Vodka
1/2 oz Rum
1/2 oz Gin
1/8 oz Orange flavored sugar-free syrup
2 oz Low carb sweet and sour

Nearly fill the glass with diet 7-Up. Top with 1/8 oz grape or raspberry flavored sugar-free syrup.

Blue Lemonade *(Low carb version)*

Carb Count: < 3.50
Tall glass, fill with ice.

1/2 oz	Vodka
1/2 oz	Rum
1/2 oz	Gin
1/4 oz	Blue ***Curacao***
2 oz	Low carb sweet and sour

Fill the glass with diet 7-Up.

Blue Lemonade #2 *(Low carb version)*

Carb Count: < 2
Tall glass, fill with ice.

1/2 oz	Vodka
1/2 oz	Rum
1/2 oz	Gin
1/8 oz	Orange flavored sugar-free syrup
2 oz	Low carb sweet and sour
2-3 drops	Blue food coloring

Fill the glass with diet 7-Up.

Electric Lemonade *(Low carb version)*

Carb Count: < 2
Tall glass, fill with ice.

1/2 oz	Vodka
1/2 oz	Rum
1/2 oz	Gin
1/8 oz	Orange flavored sugar-free syrup
2 oz	Low carb sweet and sour

Nearly fill the glass with diet 7-Up. Top with 1/2-oz tequila.

Kentucky Pink *(Low carb version)*

Carb Count: < 2
Tall glass, fill with ice.

1 oz ***Jim Beam*** Bourbon

Fill the glass with Snapple or Crystal Light Pink Lemonade.

Lemonade *(Low carb version)*

Carb Count: < 1
Tall glass, fill with ice.

1/2 oz Vodka
1/2 oz Rum
1/2 oz Gin

Fill the glass with Crystal Light Lemonade.

Lemonade #2 *(Low carb version)*

Carb Count: < 2
Tall glass, fill with ice.

1/2 oz Vodka
1/2 oz Rum
1/2 oz Gin
1/8 oz Orange flavored sugar-free syrup
2 oz Low carb sweet and sour

Fill the glass with diet 7-Up.

When verifying ID, double check the name of the issuing state. One of the most common mistakes in forged driver's licenses is misspelling the state's name. *Hello!!*

Lynchburg Lemonade *(Low carb version)*

Carb Count: < 2
Tall glass, fill with ice.

1 oz	***Jack Daniel's*** Whiskey
1/8 oz	Orange flavored sugar-free syrup
1-1/2 oz	Low carb sweet and sour

Fill the glass with diet 7-Up.

Blackberry Iced Tea *(Low carb version)*

Carb Count: < 2
Tall glass, fill with ice.

1/2 oz	Vodka
1/2 oz	Rum
1/2 oz	Gin
1/8 oz	Orange flavored sugar-free syrup
1/8 oz	Grape flavored sugar-free syrup
2 oz	Low carb sweet and sour

Fill the glass with diet Coke.

Electric Long Island Iced Tea *(Low carb version)*

Carb Count: < 2
Tall glass, fill with ice.

1/2 oz	Vodka
1/2 oz	Rum
1/2 oz	Gin
1/8 oz	Orange flavored sugar-free syrup
2 oz	Low carb sweet and sour

Nearly fill the glass with diet Coke. Top with 1/2 oz tequila.

Florida Iced Tea *(Low carb version)*

Carb Count: < 5
Tall glass, fill with ice.

1/2 oz Vodka
1/2 oz Rum
1/2 oz Gin
1/8 oz Orange flavored sugar-free syrup
1 oz Low carb sweet and sour
1 oz Orange juice

Fill the glass with sparkling water or Crystal Light Pineapple-Orange drink.

Green Apple Iced Tea *(Low carb version)*

Carb Count: < 3.50
Tall glass, fill with ice.

1/2 oz Vodka
1/2 oz Rum
1/2 oz Gin
1/8 oz Orange flavored sugar-free syrup
1/4 oz ***Sour Apple Puckers***
1-1/2 oz Low carb sweet and sour

Fill the glass with diet Coke.

In 1933, the famous Budweiser Clydesdales were introduced. These beautiful horses have been credited with re-establishing the popularity of the draft horse in America today.

Green Apple Iced Tea #2 *(Low carb version)*

Carb Count: < 2
Tall glass, fill with ice.

1/2 oz	Vodka
1/2 oz	Rum
1/2 oz	Gin
1/8 oz	Orange flavored sugar-free syrup
1/8 oz	Sour Apple flavored sugar-free syrup
1-1/2 oz	Low carb sweet and sour

Fill the glass with diet Coke.

Long Beach Iced Tea *(Low carb version)*

Carb Count: < 3
Tall glass, fill with ice.

1/2 oz	Vodka
1/2 oz	Rum
1/2 oz	Gin
1/8 oz	Orange flavored sugar-free syrup
1 oz	Low carb sweet and sour
1 oz	Cranberry juice

Fill the glass with diet Coke.

Long Island Iced Tea *(Low carb version)*

Carb Count: < 2
Tall glass, fill with ice.

1/2 oz	Vodka
1/2 oz	Rum
1/2 oz	Gin
1/8 oz	Orange flavored sugar-free syrup
2 oz	Low carb sweet and sour

Fill the glass with diet Coke.

Miami Vice Tea *(Low carb version)*

Carb Count: < 2

Tall glass, fill with ice.

1/2 oz	Gin
1 oz	Vodka
1/8 oz	Orange flavored sugar-free syrup
1/8 oz	Peach flavored sugar-free syrup
1 oz	Low carb sweet and sour

Fill the glass with diet 7-Up.

Miami Vice Tea #2 *(Low carb version)*

Carb Count: < 2

Tall glass, fill with ice.

1/2 oz	Gin
1 oz	Vodka
1/4 oz	Peach Schnapps
2 oz	Snapple sugar-free peach tea

Fill the glass with diet 7-Up.

Manhattan Iced Tea *(Low carb version)*

Carb Count: < 2

Tall glass, fill with ice.

1/2 oz	***Maker's Mark*** Bourbon
1/2 oz	Scotch
1/2 oz	Tequila
1/8 oz	Orange flavored sugar-free syrup
1 oz	Low carb sweet and sour

Fill the glass with diet Coke.

Malibu Melon Iced Tea *(Low carb version)*

Carb Count: < 2
Tall glass, fill with ice.

3/4 oz	Vodka
3/4 oz	*Malibu* Coconut Rum
1/8 oz	Orange flavored sugar-free syrup
1/8 oz	Melon flavored sugar-free syrup
1-1/2 oz	Low carb sweet and sour

Fill the glass with diet Coke.

Peach Iced Tea *(Low carb version)*

Carb Count: < 3.75
Tall glass, fill with ice.

3/4 oz	Vodka
1/2 oz	Rum
1/2 oz	Gin
1/8 oz	Orange flavored sugar-free syrup
1/4 oz	Peach Schnapps
1-1/2 oz	Low carb sweet and sour

Fill the glass with diet Coke.

Peach Iced Tea #2 *(Low carb version)*

Carb Count: < 2
Tall glass, fill with ice.

3/4 oz	Vodka
1/2 oz	Rum
1/2 oz	Gin
1/8 oz	Orange flavored sugar-free syrup
1/8 oz	Peach flavored sugar-free syrup
1-1/2 oz	Low carb sweet and sour

Fill the glass with diet Coke.

Raspberries 'n Cream Iced Tea *(Low carb version)*

Carb Count: < 3
Tall glass, fill with ice.

3/4 oz	***Smirnoff Raspberry Twist*** Vodka
1/2 oz	Rum
1/2 oz	Gin
1/8 oz	Orange flavored sugar-free syrup
1/8 oz	Raspberry flavored sugar-free syrup
1-1/2 oz	Atkins Advantage Strawberry Supreme Shake

Fill the glass with diet Coke.
This drink may foam up a bit. It helps to add the diet Coke slowly. Stirring as you add the Coke may also help.

Raspberry Iced Tea *(Low carb version)*

Carb Count: < 2
Tall glass, fill with ice.

3/4 oz	***Smirnoff Raspberry Twist*** Vodka
1/2 oz	Rum
1/2 oz	Gin
1/8 oz	Orange flavored sugar-free syrup
1/8 oz	Raspberry flavored sugar-free syrup
1-1/2 oz	Low carb strawberry margarita mix or Crystal Light Strawberry-Lemonade drink

Fill the glass with diet Coke.

> Worried about a "beer gut?" Try serving your beer over ice. The flavor is maintained and the carbonation is reduced. This is also an effective way to help prevent belching after knocking back a cold one!

Margaritas

Blackberry-Banana Margarita *(Low carb version)*

Carb Count: < 4.50

Bucket glass, fill with ice. Or, blend with ice and serve in a margarita glass.

1 oz	Tequila
1/8 oz	Lime juice
1/8 oz	Orange flavored sugar-free syrup
1/8 oz	Blackberry Schnapps
1/8 oz	***99 Bananas***
2 oz	Low carb margarita mix
3/4 oz	Sparkling water

Blackberry-Banana Margarita #2 *(Low carb version)*

Carb Count: < 2

Bucket glass, fill with ice. Or, blend with ice and serve in a margarita glass.

1 oz	Tequila
1/8 oz	Lime juice
1/8 oz	Orange flavored sugar-free syrup
1/8 oz	Blackberry flavored sugar-free syrup
1/8 oz	Banana flavored sugar-free syrup
2 oz	Low carb margarita mix
3/4 oz	Sparkling water

Blue Margarita ***(Low carb version)***

Carb Count: < 3.25

Bucket glass, fill with ice. Or, blend with ice and serve in a margarita glass. Salt rim if desired.

1 oz	Tequila
1/8 oz	Lime juice
1/4 oz	Blue ***Curacao***
2 oz	Low carb margarita mix
1 oz	Sparkling water

Blue Margarita #2 ***(Low carb version)***

Carb Count: < 2

Bucket glass, fill with ice. Or, blend with ice and serve in a margarita glass. Salt rim if desired.

1 oz	Tequila
1/8 oz	Lime juice
1/8 oz	Orange flavored sugar-free syrup
2 oz	Low carb margarita mix
3 drops	Blue food coloring
1 oz	Sparkling water

Cadillac Margarita ***(Low carb version)***

Carb Count: < 2.50

Bucket glass, fill with ice. Or, blend with ice and serve in a margarita glass. Salt rim if desired.

1 oz	***Jose Cuervo*** Gold Tequila
1/8 oz	Lime juice
1/8 oz	***Grand Marnier***
2 oz	Low carb margarita mix
1 oz	Sparkling water

Gold Margarita *(Low carb version)*

Carb Count: < 2

Bucket glass, fill with ice. Or, blend with ice and serve in a margarita glass. Salt rim if desired.

1 oz	***Jose Cuervo*** Gold Tequila
1/8 oz	Lime juice
1/8 oz	Orange flavored sugar-free syrup
2 oz	Low carb margarita mix
1 oz	Sparkling water

Kiwi Margarita *(Low carb version)*

Carb Count: < 2

Bucket glass, fill with ice. Or, blend with ice and serve in a margarita glass.

1 oz	Tequila
1/8 oz	Lime juice
1/8 oz	Kiwi flavored sugar-free syrup
1/8 oz	Orange flavored sugar-free syrup
2 oz	Low carb margarita mix
1 oz	Sparkling water

Margarita *(Low carb version)*

Carb Count: < 4

Bucket glass, fill with ice. Or, blend with ice and serve in a margarita glass. Salt rim if desired.

1 oz	Tequila
1/8 oz	Lime juice
1/4 oz	Triple Sec
2 oz	Low carb margarita mix
1 oz	Sparkling water

Margarita #2 ***(Low carb version)***

Carb Count: < 2

Bucket glass, fill with ice. Or, blend with ice and serve in a margarita glass. Salt rim if desired.

1 oz	Tequila
1/8 oz	Lime juice
1/8 oz	Orange flavored sugar-free syrup
2 oz	Low carb margarita mix
1 oz	Sparkling water

Peach Margarita ***(Low carb version)***

Carb Count: < 3.50

Bucket glass, fill with ice. Or, blend with ice and serve in a margarita glass.

1 oz	Tequila
1/4 oz	Peach Schnapps
1/8 oz	***Grand Marnier***
2 oz	Low carb margarita mix
1 oz	Sparkling water

Peach Margarita #2 ***(Low carb version)***

Carb Count: < 2

Bucket glass, fill with ice. Or, blend with ice and serve in a margarita glass.

1 oz	Tequila
1/8 oz	Lime juice
1/8 oz	Peach flavored sugar-free syrup
1/8 oz	Orange flavored sugar-free syrup
2 oz	Low carb margarita mix
1 oz	Sparkling water

Raspberry Margarita *(Low carb version)*

Carb Count: < 2

Bucket glass, fill with ice. Or, blend with ice and serve in a margarita glass.

1 oz Tequila
1/8 oz Lime juice
1/8 oz Raspberry flavored sugar-free syrup
1/8 oz Orange flavored sugar-free syrup
2 oz Low carb strawberry margarita mix
1 oz Sparkling water

Strawberry Margarita *(Low carb version)*

Carb Count: < 2

Bucket glass, fill with ice. Or, blend with ice and serve in a margarita glass.

1 oz Tequila
1/8 oz Lime juice
1/8 oz Strawberry flavored sugar-free syrup
1/8 oz Orange flavored sugar-free syrup
2 oz Low carb strawberry margarita mix
1 oz Sparkling water

Watermelon Margarita *(Low carb version)*

Carb Count: < 2

Bucket glass, fill with ice. Or, blend with ice and serve in a margarita glass.

1 oz Tequila
1/8 oz Lime juice
1/8 oz Watermelon flavored sugar-free syrup
1/8 oz Orange flavored sugar-free syrup
2 oz Low carb margarita mix
1 oz Sparkling water

Martinis and Manhattans

Martinis and Gibsons are made with gin or vodka.

Manhattans are traditionally made with bourbon, but many times other whiskeys are used.

A Manhattan made with scotch is often called a Rob Roy.

Call names for the liquors may be used:

Absolut Martini
Tanqueray Martini
Johnny Walker Rob Roy
Bushmill's Manhattan
Grey Goose Gibson

- **On the Rocks** – Serve in a rocks glass filled with ice. Add the Vermouth, then add the main liquor.
- **Straight Up** – Serve in a chilled martini glass, no ice. In a mixing glass add 1 cup of ice and the Vermouth. Next, add the main liquor. Shake or stir, and strain into a chilled martini glass.
- The more "dry" the martini, the less Dry Vermouth is used.
- For a "dirty martini," add about 1/4 oz olive juice (from the green olives) to the drink after mixing, before serving.
- A Gibson is the same as a Martini with a pearl onion instead of an olive.

Martini

Carb Count: < 1
Martini glass, chilled. Shake and strain:

4-6 Drops	**DRY** Vermouth
2 oz	Gin or Vodka

Garnish with a green olive on a spear or pick.

Dry Martini

Carb Count: < 1
Martini glass, chilled. Shake and strain:

2-4 Drops	**DRY** Vermouth
2 oz	Gin or Vodka

Garnish with a green olive on a spear or pick.

Extra Dry Martini

Carb Count: < 1
Martini glass, chilled. Shake and strain:

1-2 Drops	**DRY** Vermouth
2 oz	Gin or Vodka

Garnish with a green olive on a spear or pick.

Extra Extra Dry Martini

Carb Count: < 1
Martini glass, chilled. Shake and strain:

0-1 Drops	**DRY** Vermouth
2 oz	Gin or Vodka

Garnish with a green olive on a spear or pick.

Gibson

Carb Count: < 1
Martini glass, chilled. Shake and strain:

4-6 Drops	**DRY** Vermouth
2 oz	Gin or Vodka

Garnish with a pearl onion on a spear or pick.

Dry Gibson

Carb Count: < 1
Martini glass, chilled. Shake and strain:

2-4 Drops	**DRY** Vermouth
2 oz	Gin or Vodka

Garnish with a pearl onion on a spear or pick.

Extra Dry Gibson

Carb Count: < 1
Martini glass, chilled. Shake and strain:

1-2 Drops	**DRY** Vermouth
2 oz	Gin or Vodka

Garnish with a pearl onion on a spear or pick.

Extra Extra Dry Gibson

Carb Count: < 1
Martini glass, chilled. Shake and strain:

0-1 Drops	**DRY** Vermouth
2 oz	Gin or Vodka

Garnish with a pearl onion on a spear or pick.

Manhattan

Carb Count: < 1.50

Martini glass, chilled. Shake and strain:

1/4 oz **SWEET** Vermouth
2 oz Bourbon

Garnish with a cherry.

Dry Manhattan

Carb Count: < 1

Martini glass, chilled. Shake and strain:

1/4 oz **DRY** Vermouth
2 oz Bourbon

Garnish with a green olive on a spear or pick.

Perfect Manhattan

Carb Count: < 1.25

Martini glass, chilled. Shake and strain:

1/8 oz **SWEET** Vermouth
1/8 oz **DRY** Vermouth
2 oz Bourbon

Garnish with a lemon twist.

SoCo Manhattan

Carb Count: < 6

Martini glass, chilled. Shake and strain:

1/4 oz **DRY** Vermouth
2 oz ***Southern Comfort***

Garnish with a cherry.

Apple-Tini *(Low carb version)*

Carb Count: < 3
Martini glass, chilled.
Shake with ice and strain:

3/4 oz ***Crown Royal*** Whiskey
1/4 oz ***Sour Apple Puckers***
1/4 oz Cranberry juice
1/2 oz Low carb sweet and sour

Berry-Tini *(Low carb version)*

Carb Count: < 3
Martini glass, chilled.
Shake with ice and strain:

3/4 oz Raspberry Vodka
1/4 oz ***Chambord***
1/4 oz Cranberry juice
1/2 oz Low carb sweet and sour

007 Vodka Martini

Carb Count: < 1

This drink was made famous in the MGM/UA movie, ***Dr. No***, starring Sean Connery.

"A vodka martini. Shaken, not stirred."
James Bond 007

Champagne goblet, chilled. Shake and strain:

1-1/2 oz ***Gordon's*** Gin
1/2 oz Vodka
1/4 oz ***Kina Lillet*** Dry Vermouth

Garnish with a thin slice of lemon peel.

Lemon Drop *(Low carb version)*

Carb Count: < 2
Martini glass, chilled.
Shake and strain:

1-1/2 oz	Lemon Vodka
1/8 oz	Orange flavored sugar-free syrup
1/4 oz	Fresh lemon juice

Garnish with a lemon slice.

Red Headed Slut *(Low carb version)*

Carb Count: < 5.50
Martini glass, chilled.
Shake with ice and strain:

3/4 oz	Vodka
1/4 oz	***Jagermeister***
1/4 oz	Peach Schnapps
1/4 oz	Cranberry juice
1/4 oz	Low carb sweet and sour

Sources for the 007 Martini/Mojito/Mint Julep:

"Drink Like 007," *M16 – The Home of 007*, 26th November 2002, <http://www.mi6.co.uk/sections/ articles/drink_ like_007.php3?t=&s=articles>, (5 May 2004).
If you are a James Bond fan, you absolutely must see this site.

"Make Mine a 007 – The James Bond Films," *The Minister of Martinis*, 2002, <http://home.earthlink.net/~atomic_rom/007 /films.htm>, (5 May 2004).

"Why did James Bond want his martinis shaken, not stirred?," *The Straight Dope*, 28-Nov-2000, <http://www.straightdope.com/ mailbag/mmartini.html>, (5 May 2004).

Coffee and Tea Drinks

***Bailey's* Coffee** *(Low carb version)*

Carb Count: < 8

Large coffee cup, warmed. 1/2 fill with coffee.

1 oz ***Bailey's*** Irish Cream

Fill the cup with fresh, hot coffee.

Brandy Coffee *(Low carb version)*

Carb Count: < 3

Large coffee cup, warmed.

1 oz ***Hennessy*** Cognac

Fill the cup with coffee.

Candlelight Coffee *(Low carb version)*

Carb Count: < 7

Large coffee cup, warmed.

1/2 oz Peach Schnapps
1/2 oz Crème de Noyaux (Almond)
1 oz ***Bacardi*** 151 Rum

Fill the cup with fresh, hot coffee.

Stale coffee can cause the Irish Cream to curdle.

Caramel Apples *(Low carb version)*

Carb Count: < 7

Large coffee cup, warmed.

1/2 oz Apple Schnapps (not ***Puckers***)
1/2 oz Butterscotch Schnapps

Fill the cup with hot tea or coffee.

Caramel Nudge *(Low carb version)*

Carb Count: < 6.25

Large coffee cup, warmed.

1/4 oz ***Kahlua***
1/4 oz Butterscotch Schnapps

Fill the cup with fresh, hot coffee.

Coffee Bitch *(Low carb version)*

Carb Count: < 2.75

Large coffee cup, warmed. 1/2 fill with coffee.

1/4 oz ***Bailey's*** Irish Cream
1 oz Whiskey

Fill the cup with fresh, hot coffee.

Coffee Calypso *(Low carb version)*

Carb Count: < 6.50

Large coffee cup, warmed.

1/2 oz ***Kahlua***
1 oz Rum

Fill the cup with fresh, hot coffee.

Coffee Calypso #2 *(Low carb version)*

Carb Count: < 1
Large coffee cup, warmed.

1/8 oz ***Kahlua*** flavored sugar-free syrup
1-1/4 oz Rum

Fill the cup with fresh, hot coffee.

French Coffee *(Low carb version)*

Carb Count: < 5
Large coffee cup, warmed.

1/2 oz ***Grand Marnier***
1/2 oz ***Courvoisier*** Cognac

Fill the cup with fresh, hot coffee.

Irish Coffee *(Low carb version)*

Carb Count: < 1
Large coffee cup, warmed.

1 oz Irish Whiskey

Fill the cup with fresh, hot coffee.

Jamaican Coffee *(Low carb version)*

Carb Count: < 1
Large coffee cup, warmed.

1 oz ***Myers'*** Rum

Fill the cup with fresh, hot coffee.

Kioki Calypso *(Low carb version)*

Carb Count: < 5.75
Large coffee cup, warmed.

1/4 oz ***Kahlua***
1 oz Brandy
1/8 oz Chocolate flavored sugar-free syrup

Fill the cup with fresh, hot coffee.

Mexican Coffee *(Low carb version)*

Carb Count: < 3.75
Large coffee cup, warmed.

1/4 oz ***Kahlua***
1 oz Tequila

Fill the cup with fresh, hot coffee.

Peach Tea Warm-up *(Low carb version)*

Carb Count: < 4.50
Large coffee cup, warmed.

1/4 oz Peach Schnapps
1 oz Cognac

Fill the cup with hot peach tea. This recipe is also good as an iced tea.

The famous 007 Martini was originally called a "Vesper" in the book ***Casino Royale***, by Ian Fleming.

Raspberry Tea *(Low carb version)*

Carb Count: < 5.50
Large coffee cup, warmed.

1/4 oz ***Chambord***
1 oz Brandy

Fill the cup with hot raspberry tea. For an iced tea try using Crystal Light Raspberry drink.

Scottish Coffee *(Low carb version)*

Carb Count: < 1
Large coffee cup, warmed.

1 oz Scotch

Fill the cup with fresh, hot coffee.

Scottish Tea *(Low carb version)*

Carb Count: < 1
Large coffee cup, warmed.

1 oz Scotch

Fill the cup with hot lemon flavored tea. This is also good as an iced tea.

Ski Lift *(Low carb version)*

Carb Count: < 4.75
Large coffee cup, warmed.

1 oz ***E & J*** Cognac
1/4 oz Peppermint Schnapps

Fill the cup with fresh, hot coffee.

Ski Lift #2 *(Low carb version)*

Carb Count: < 8
Large coffee cup, warmed.

1 oz ***Kahlua***
1/4 oz Peppermint Schnapps

Fill the cup with fresh, hot coffee.

Southern Hospitali-Tea *(Low carb version)*

Carb Count: < 3.50
Large coffee cup, warmed.

1 oz ***Southern Comfort***

Fill the cup with hot tea. Garnish with a lemon wedge.

Spanish Coffee *(Low carb version)*

Carb Count: < 1
Large coffee cup, warmed.

1 oz Tequila

Fill the cup with fresh, hot coffee.

Overheard in the bar:

"So I said to the IRS agent…"

"I can't list my girlfriend as a dependent?" (This question was asked while the man's wife was sitting beside him.)

"Can I count justifiable homicide as a deduction?" (Asked by the wife of the man in the comment above.)

Shooters

There are several ways to make beautifully layers shooters. The most important thing is to slow the rate that the liqueur pours into the shot glass, to keep the layers from mixing. It is hard to free pour while doing this, so use your eye and make a "best guess" as to when you have added enough.

1. **Cherries**

   Pour the bottom layer of liqueur into a shot glass. Suspend the cherry over the shot glass, holding it by the stem. Slowly pour the next layer of liqueur over the cherry, slowing the rate the liqueur pours into the glass. Pour the next layer in the same fashion.

   If you are going to give the cherry to your customer, set it in a separate shot glass. If you set it in the layered shooter you just made, the weight of the cherry will mess up the look of the drink.

   It is not acceptable to eat the cherry yourself, while you are working.

2. **Spoons**

   Pour the bottom layer of liqueur into a shot glass. While holding a spoon by the handle, slowly pour the next layer over the back of the spoon. Pour the next layer in the same fashion. Resist the temptation to lick the spoon.

3. **Using the side of the glass**

   Pour the bottom layer of liqueur into a shot glass. While tipping the glass about 30 degrees, slowly pour the next layer. The liqueur should slide down the side of the glass and float on the previous layer. This method leaves a "trail" down the side of the glass, spoiling the layered look on one side, but, is good to know if you are in a hurry and don't have a spoon or cherry handy.

For best results, pour the heaviest layers first, such as ***Kahlua*** and ***Bailey's*** Irish Cream. Of the two, ***Kahlua*** should always be poured first.

Apple Cream *(Low carb version)*

Carb Count: < 2.25
Shot glass, no ice.

1 oz	Vanilla Rum or Vanilla Vodka
1/4 oz	Apple Schnapps

Apple Betty *(Low carb version)*

Carb Count: < 4
Shot glass, no ice.

1/4 oz	***Bailey's*** Irish Cream
1/4 oz	Apple Schnapps
3/4 oz	Vodka

Apple Pie *(Low carb version)*

Carb Count: < 2.50
Shot glass, no ice. Layer:

1/4 oz	***Bailey's*** Irish Cream (bottom)
Splash	Sour Apple flavored sugar-free syrup (next)
3/4 oz	Vodka (next)
1/4 oz	***Goldschlager*** (top)

Berry Blast *(Low carb version)*

Carb Count: < 3
Shot glass, no ice.

1 oz	Raspberry Rum
1/4 oz	***Chambord***

B-52 *(Low carb version)*

Carb Count: < 6.50
Shot glass, no ice. Layer:

1/4 oz	***Kahlua*** (bottom)
1/4 oz	***Bailey's*** Irish Cream (middle)
1/4 oz	Orange Vodka (middle)
1/4 oz	***Grand Marnier*** (top)

B-52 #2 *(Low carb version)*

Carb Count: < 4.75
Shot glass, no ice. Layer:

1/4 oz	***Kahlua*** (bottom)
1/4 oz	***Bailey's*** Irish Cream (middle)
1 oz	Orange Vodka (middle)
Splash	Orange flavored sugar-free syrup (top)

Boy Toy *(Low carb version)*

Carb Count: < 2.50
Shot glass, no ice.

3/4 oz	Light Rum
1/4 oz	***Southern Comfort***
1/4 oz	Blackberry Schnapps

Buttery Nipple *(Low carb version)*

Carb Count: < 7.25
Shot glass, no ice. Layer:

1/4 oz	***Bailey's*** Irish Cream (bottom)
3/4 oz	Vanilla Vodka (middle)
1/2 oz	Butterscotch Schnapps (top)

Buttery Nipple #2 *(Low carb version)*

Carb Count: < 2
Shot glass, no ice.

1 oz	Vanilla Vodka
1/4 oz	***Bailey's*** Irish Cream
1/8 oz	Caramel flavored sugar-free syrup

Caramel Apple Pie *(Low carb version)*

Carb Count: < 7.50
Shot glass, no ice. Layer:

1/4 oz	***Bailey's*** Irish Cream (bottom)
Splash	Apple flavored sugar-free syrup (next)
1/2 oz	Vanilla Vodka (next)
1/4 oz	Butterscotch Schnapps (next)
1/4 oz	***Goldschlager*** (top)

Caramel Strawberries *(Low carb version)*

Carb Count: < 2.25
Shot glass, no ice. Layer:

1/4 oz	Atkins Advantage Strawberry Supreme Shake, ***chilled*** (bottom)
1/4 oz	Butterscotch Schnapps (middle)
3/4 oz	Vanilla Vodka (top)

Caramel Berries *(Low carb version)*

Carb Count: < 2.25
Shot glass, no ice. Layer:

1/4 oz	Atkins Advantage Strawberry Supreme Shake, ***chilled*** (bottom)
1/4 oz	Butterscotch Schnapps (middle)
3/4 oz	Raspberry Rum (top)

Chocolate Cake *(Low carb version)*

Carb Count: < 3
Shot glass, no ice.

3/4 oz ***Absolut Citron*** Vodka
1/4 oz ***Frangelico***

Serve with several lemon slices dipped in sugar substitute.

Christmas Cactus *(Low carb version)*

Carb Count: < 2
Shot glass, no ice.

1/2 oz Vodka
1/2 oz Tequila
1/4 oz Peppermint Schnapps

Christmas Cookie *(Low carb version)*

Carb Count: < 4.75
Shot glass, no ice.

3/4 oz Vanilla Vodka
1/4 oz ***Goldschlager***
1/4 oz ***Bailey's*** Irish Cream

Cinnamon Apple *(Low carb version)*

Carb Count: < 2.50
Shot glass, no ice.

1 oz Vodka
1/8 oz Apple Schnapps
1/8 oz ***Goldschlager***

Cinnamon Snap *(Low carb version)*

Carb Count: < 2.85
Shot glass, no ice.

1 oz Vodka
1/4 oz ***Goldschlager***

Coconut Coffee *(Low carb version)*

Carb Count: < 3
Shot glass, no ice.

1 oz Coconut Rum
1/4 oz ***Frangelico***

Cranberry Cheesecake *(Low carb version)*

Carb Count: < 1
Shot glass, no ice.

1 oz Vanilla Vodka
1/4 oz Cranberry juice

Damn Hot Stuff *(Low carb version)*

Carb Count: < 3
Shot glass, no ice.

1 oz Vodka
1/4 oz Cinnamon Schnapps
2-3 drops Tabasco Sauce

Duck Farts *(Low carb version)*

Carb Count: < 4.75
Shot glass, no ice. Layer:

1/4 oz ***Kahlua*** (bottom)
1/4 oz ***Bailey's*** Irish Cream (middle)
3/4 oz ***Crown Royal*** Whiskey (top)

Elephant Farts *(Low carb version)*

Carb Count: < 1
Shot glass, no ice.

3/4 oz ***Jack Daniel's*** Whiskey
1/4 oz ***Bacardi*** 151 Rum
*** Flaming is NOT recommended!

Fuzzy Bush *(Low carb version)*

Carb Count: < 2
Shot glass, no ice.

3/4 oz ***Bushmill's*** Irish Whiskey
1/4 oz Peach Schnapps

German Chocolate Cake *(Low carb version)*

Carb Count: < 7.50
Shot glass, no ice. Layer:

1/4 oz ***Kahlua*** (bottom)
1/4 oz ***Bailey's*** Irish Cream (middle)
1/2 oz Vanilla Vodka (middle)
1/4 oz ***Frangelico*** (top)

German Chocolate Cake #2 *(Low carb version)*

Carb Count: < 4.75
Shot glass, no ice.

1/4 oz ***Kahlua***
1/4 oz ***Bailey's*** Irish Cream
3/4 oz Vanilla Vodka
1/8 oz Hazelnut flavored sugar-free syrup

Going Bananas *(Low carb version)*

Carb Count: < 2.25
Shot glass, no ice.

1 oz Banana Rum
1/4 oz ***99 Bananas***

Gold Rush *(Low carb version)*

Carb Count: < 1.50
Shot glass, no ice.

3/4 oz ***Jim Beam*** Bourbon
1/2 oz ***Southern Comfort***

Gorilla Fart *(Low carb version)*

Carb Count: < 1
Shot glass, no ice.

3/4 oz ***Wild Turkey*** Bourbon
1/2 oz ***Bacardi*** 151 Rum
*** Flaming is NOT recommended!

Harley Davidson *(Low carb version)*

Carb Count: = 2.75
Shot glass, no ice.

3/4 oz ***Jack Daniel's*** Whiskey
1/4 oz ***Yukon Jack*** Whiskey

Hawaiian Tapdance *(Low carb version)*

Carb Count: < 1.50
Shot glass, no ice.

3/4 oz ***Malibu*** Coconut Rum
1/2 oz ***Southern Comfort***

Hot Tamale *(Low carb version)*

Carb Count: < 3
Shot glass, no ice.

1 oz	Gold Tequila
1/4 oz	***Goldschlager***

Italian Stallion *(Low carb version)*

Carb Count: < 3
Shot glass, no ice.

1 oz	Scotch
1/4 oz	***Galliano***

Jager-Mint Mudslide *(Low carb version)*

Carb Count: = 5.50
Shot glass, no ice.

1/4 oz	***Jagermeister***
1/4 oz	***Rumplemintz***
3/4 oz	***Wild Turkey*** Bourbon

Jamaican Bobsled *(Low carb version)*

Carb Count: < 2
Shot glass, no ice.

1 oz	***Myers'*** Rum
1/4 oz	Peppermint Schnapps

Kamakazi *(Low carb version)*

Carb Count: < 2
Shot glass, no ice. Garnish with a lime slice.

1-1/4 oz	Vodka
1/8 oz	Orange flavored sugar-free syrup
Splash	Lime juice

Key Lime Pie *(Low carb version)*

Carb Count: < 2.75
Shot glass, no ice. Serve with a lime slice.

3/4 oz ***Smirnoff Lime Twist*** Vodka
1/4 oz ***Stoli*** Vanilla Vodka
1/4 oz Butterscotch Schnapps

Laser Beam *(Low carb version)*

Carb Count: < 3
Shot glass, no ice.

1 oz Tequila
1/4 oz ***Galliano***

Lemon Meringue Pie *(Low carb version)*

Carb Count: < 2.75
Shot glass, no ice. Serve with a lemon slice.

3/4 oz ***Absolut Citron*** Vodka
1/4 oz ***Stoli*** Vanilla Vodka
1/4 oz Butterscotch Schnapps

Licorice Twist *(Low carb version)*

Carb Count: < 3
Shot glass, no ice.

1 oz Vodka
1/4 oz ***Sambuca***

> The name vodka comes from the Russian word "voda," meaning "the little water of life."

Liquid Cocaine *(Low carb version)*

Carb Count: < 5.75
Shot glass, no ice. Layer:

1/4 oz ***Jagermeister*** (bottom)
1/4 oz ***Rumplemintz*** (middle)
3/4 oz ***Bacardi*** 151 Rum (top)

Liquid Cocaine #2 *(Low carb version)*

Carb Count: < 3
Shot glass, no ice. Layer:

1/4 oz ***Jagermeister*** (bottom)
1/8 oz Peppermint flavored sugar-free syrup (next)
1/4 oz Rum
3/4 oz ***Bacardi*** 151 Rum (top)

Marabou *(Low carb version)*

Carb Count: < 4.50
Shot glass, no ice.

3/4 oz Gold Rum
1/4 oz Butterscotch Schnapps
1/4 oz ***Grand Marnier***

Melon Madness *(Low carb version)*

Carb Count: < 3
Shot glass, no ice.

1 oz Coconut Rum
1/4 oz ***Midori***

Mexican Coffee *(Low carb version)*

Carb Count: < 3
Shot glass, no ice.

1 oz	Tequila
1/4 oz	***Frangelico***

Mind Eraser *(Low carb version)*

Carb Count: < 3
Rocks glass, fill with ice.

1/4 oz	***Kahlua***
3/4 oz	Vodka

Top with club soda.

Monkey Farts *(Low carb version)*

Carb Count: < 4.75
Shot glass, no ice. Layer:

1/4 oz	***Kahlua*** (bottom)
1/4 oz	***Bailey's*** Irish Cream (middle)
3/4 oz	Vodka (middle)
Splash	Banana flavored sugar-free syrup (top)

Mud Slide *(Low carb version)*

Carb Count: < 4.75
Shot glass, no ice. Layer:

1/4 oz	***Kahlua*** (bottom)
1/4 oz	***Bailey's*** Irish Cream (middle)
3/4 oz	Vodka (top)

Oatmeal Cookie ***(Low carb version)***

Carb Count: < 6.25
Shot glass, no ice. Layer:

1/4 oz ***Kahlua*** (bottom)
1/4 oz ***Bailey's*** Irish Cream (next)
3/4 oz Vodka (next)
1/8 oz Caramel flavored sugar-free syrup (next)
1/8 oz ***Goldschlager*** (top)

Oatmeal Cookie 2 ***(Low carb version)***

Carb Count: < 6.25
Shot glass, no ice. Layer:

1/4 oz ***Jagermeister*** (bottom)
1/4 oz ***Bailey's*** Irish Cream (next)
3/4 oz Vodka (next)
1/8 oz Caramel flavored sugar-free syrup (next)
1/8 oz ***Goldschlager*** (top)

What is tequila made from? Tequila is distilled from the sap of the Blue Agave plant. Contrary to popular belief, the Blue Agave is not a cactus, but rather a cousin to the lily and the amaryllis. The Blue Agave is also known as the American Aloe. To be labeled as tequila, the liquor must be distilled in the city of Tequila, Mexico. Tequilas made elsewhere in Mexico are called Mescal or Mezcal.

Tequila may be silver or gold. The golden color comes from aging in used whiskey barrels.

Orange Tango *(Low carb version)*

Carb Count: < 2

Shot glass, no ice.

1 oz Gold Rum

1/4 oz ***Grand Marnier***

Panty Knot *(Low carb version)*

Carb Count: < 5.25

Shot glass, no ice.

Shake and strain:

1/2 oz Vanilla Vodka

1/2 oz Pear Brandy

1/4 oz Peach Schnapps

Peachy Keen *(Low carb version)*

Carb Count: < 2.25

Shot glass, no ice.

1/4 oz Atkins Advantage Strawberry Supreme Shake, ***chilled*** (bottom)

1/4 oz Peach Schnapps (middle)

1 oz Raspberry Rum (top)

Peach Pie *(Low carb version)*

Carb Count: < 2.50

Shot glass, no ice.

1 oz Vodka

1/8 oz Peach Schnapps

1/8 oz ***Goldschlager***

Peppermint Paddy *(Low carb version)*

Carb Count: < 2
Shot glass, no ice.

1 oz Vanilla Rum or Vanilla Vodka
1/4 oz Peppermint Schnapps

Pink Russian *(Low carb version)*

Carb Count: < 4.75
Shot glass, no ice.

1 oz Vanilla Vodka
1/4 oz ***Tequila Rose*** Strawberry Tequila
1/4 oz Kahlua

Pink Russian #2 *Low carb version)*

Carb Count: < 2.25
Shot glass, no ice. Layer:

1/4 oz ***Tequila Rose*** Strawberry Tequila
1/2 oz Atkins Advantage Chocolate Shake (*chilled*)
1 oz Vanilla Vodka

Pineapple Upside Down Cake *(Low carb version)*

Carb Count: < 1.50
Shot glass, chilled, no ice.
Shake with ice and strain:

1/4 oz Pineapple juice
1 oz ***Stoli*** Vanilla Vodka
Splash Cherry flavored sugar-free syrup

Prairie Fire *(Low carb version)*

Carb Count: < 1.50
Shot glass, no ice.

1 oz Tequila

Top with red or green Tabasco Sauce.

Purple People *(Low carb version)*

Carb Count: < 3
Shot glass, no ice.

1 oz Raspberry Vodka
1/8 oz ***Chambord***
1/8 oz ***Sambuca***

Silk Panties *(Low carb version)*

Carb Count: < 1
Shot glass, no ice.

1 oz Vodka
1/8 oz Peach flavored sugar-free syrup
1/8 oz Sparkling water

Silk Panties #2 *(Low carb version)*

Carb Count: < 2
Shot glass, no ice.

1 oz Vodka
1/4 oz Peach Schnapps

Where does bourbon come from? Bourbon County, Kentucky, USA. Bourbon, a member of the whiskey family, is made from a variety of grains, and must contain at least 51% corn.

Tennessee Two Step *(Low carb version)*

Carb Count: < 1
Shot glass, no ice.

1 oz	***Jack Daniel's*** Whiskey
1/4 oz	***Southern Comfort***

Tijuana Hot Spot *(Low carb version)*

Carb Count: < 3
Shot glass, no ice.

1 oz	Tequila
1/4 oz	Cinnamon Schnapps
2-3 drops	Tabasco Sauce

Torpedo *(Low carb version)*

Carb Count: < 2
Shot glass, no ice.

1-1/4 oz	Tequila
Splash	Bloody Mary mix
2–3 Drops	Tabasco Sauce

24 Karat Nightmare *(Low carb version)*

Carb Count: = 8.25
Shot glass, no ice.

1/4 oz	***Jagermeister***
1/4 oz	***Rumplemintz***
1/4 oz	***Goldschlager***
1/2 oz	Vodka

Twist and Shout *(Low carb version)*

Carb Count: < 2
Shot glass, no ice.

1/2 oz 151 Rum
1/2 oz Tequila
1/4 oz Peach Schnapps
*** Flaming is NOT recommended!

Washington Apple *(Low carb version)*

Carb Count: < 5.
Shot glass, no ice.

3/4 oz ***Southern Comfort***
1/4 oz ***Sour Apple Puckers***
1/4 oz Cranberry juice

Washington Apple #2 *(Low carb version)*

Carb Count: < 3
Shot glass, no ice.

3/4 oz ***Crown Royal*** Whiskey
1/4 oz ***Sour Apple Puckers***
1/4 oz Cranberry juice

Standing six feet tall at the shoulder and weighing between 2,000 and 2,300 pounds, the Budweiser Clydesdales are an impressive display of sheer horsepower.

More than 35 Clydesdale mares, stallions and foals are kept at the famous Budweiser Clydesdale Stables. These stables are visited by thousands of people every year.

Kickin' Jell-O Shooters

Jell-O shooters are fun to make and even more fun to eat. Bring them out as a playful addition to a party, or keep them handy to serve if the evening needs a little jump start to get going.

Shooters have a practical side as well. They are a great way to move liquor that has been sitting around for a while, giving you a chance to rotate your stock, and use up the little bits and dabs of liquor you have left in the bottle.

To stay low carb, do not use cream liquors, cordials, brandies, cognacs, schnapps or anything that starts with "Crème de."

The alcohol in the shooters is not burned off.

Consider 4 Jell-O shooters as equal to drinking a full shot of 86 proof liquor.

Jell-O Shooters *(Low carb version)*

Carb Count: < 1

1 box	Sugar-Free Jell-O (any flavor)
2/3 cup	Vodka (or other hard liquor)
1 cup	Hot water

Make the Jell-O according the instructions on the box. Replace the cold water with the liquor. Pour the mix into small Dixie cups or other small plastic cups. Chill until firm. Serve cold.

For best results, each liquor should have it's own flavor and color. This way, if someone doesn't like whiskey, for example, they can easily recognize which shooters are made with whiskey and avoid them.

Here are some tasty ideas: tequila with lime Jell-O, vodka with grape, rum with peach, and gin with black cherry.

Jell-O Shooters 2 (Party Mix) *(Low carb version)*

Carb Count: < 1

3 boxes	Sugar-Free Jell-O
2 cups	Vodka (or other hard liquor)
3 cups	Hot water

Make the Jell-O according the instructions on the box. Replace the cold water with the liquor. Stir for about a minute. Pour into small Dixie cups, or small plastic condiment containers. Serve cold.

Long Island Jell-O Shooters *(Low carb version)*

Carb Count: < 1

This recipe is made in layers. Each layer is made with a different liquor.

1 box	Sugar-Free Jell-O (any flavor)
2/3 cup	Vodka (replaces the cold water)
1 cup	Hot water

Boil the water. Add the Jell-O, stirring constantly. After the Jell-O has dissolved, stir for another 2 minutes, then add the vodka. Stir for about a minute. Pour 1/2" deep into small Dixie cups, or small plastic condiment containers. Allow to set-up in the refrigerator until slightly firm, about 15 minutes

Next,

1 box	Sugar-Free Lemon-Lime Jell-O
2/3 cup	Gin
1 cup	Hot water

Boil the water. Add the Jell-O, stirring constantly. After the Jell-O has dissolved, stir for another 2 minutes, then add the gin. Stir for about a minute. Pour 1/2" deep on top of the vodka Jell-O. Allow the Jell-O to set-up in the refrigerator until slightly firm, about 15 minutes.

Next,

1 box	Sugar-Free Orange Jell-O
2/3 cup	Rum (replaces the cold water)
1 cup	Hot water

Boil the water. Add the Jell-O, stirring constantly. After the Jell-O has dissolved, stir for another 2 minutes, then add the rum. Stir for about a minute. Pour 1/2" deep on top of the gin Jell-O. Allow the Jell-O to set-up in the refrigerator until firm. Serve and enjoy!

This fun and colorful recipe can also be made using a 9"x13" baking pan. The pan needs to be at least 2" deep. Pour the Jell-O in layers, allowing each layer to set slightly before pouring the next round. Cut into 1-1/2" squares. Serve cold.

Caribbean Jell-O Shooters *(Low carb version)*

Carb Count: < 1

This recipe is made in layers. Each layer is made with a different liquor.

1 box	Sugar-Free Jell-O (any flavor)
2/3 cup	Coconut Rum (replaces the cold water)
1 cup	Hot water

Boil the water. Add the Jell-O, stirring constantly. After the Jell-O has dissolved, stir for another 2 minutes, then add the rum. Stir for about a minute. Pour 1/2" deep into small Dixie cups, or small plastic condiment containers. Allow to set-up in the refrigerator until slightly firm, about 15 minutes

Next,

1 box	Sugar-Free Jell-O (Same flavor as above)
2/3 cup	Strawberry-Kiwi Rum
1 cup	Hot water

Boil the water. Add the Jell-O, stirring constantly. After the Jell-O has dissolved, stir for another 2 minutes, then add the rum. Stir for about a minute. Pour 1/2" deep on top of the previous Jell-O. Allow to set-up in the refrigerator for about 15 minutes, until slightly firm.

Next,

1 box	Sugar-Free Jell-O (Same flavor as above)
2/3 cup	Strawberry-Banana Rum
1 cup	Hot water

Boil the water. Add the Jell-O, stirring constantly. After the Jell-O has dissolved, stir for another 2 minutes, then add the rum. Stir for about a minute, then pour 1/2 deep on top of the previous Jell-O. Allow to set-up in the refrigerator until firm. Serve and enjoy!

This fun recipe can also be made using a 9"x13" baking pan. The pan needs to be at least 2" deep. Pour the Jell-O in layers, allowing each layer to set slightly before pouring the next round. Cut into 1-1/2" squares. Serve cold.

New Orleans Jell-O Shooters *(Low carb version)*

Carb Count: < 1

This recipe is made in layers. Each layer is made with a different liquor.

1 box	Sugar-Free Jell-O (any flavor)
2/3 cup	Lemon Vodka
1 cup	Hot water

Boil the water. Add the Jell-O, stirring constantly. After the Jell-O has dissolved, stir for another 2 minutes, then add the vodka. Stir for about a minute. Pour 1/2" deep into small Dixie cups, or small plastic condiment containers. Allow to set-up in the refrigerator until slightly firm, about 15 minutes.

Next,

1 box	Sugar-Free Jell-O (Same flavor as above)
2/3 cup	Orange Vodka
1 cup	Hot water

Boil the water and add the Jell-O, stirring constantly. After the Jell-O has dissolved, stir for another 2 minutes, then add the vodka. Stir for about a minute, then pour 1/2" deep on top of the previous Jell-O. Allow to set-up in the refrigerator until slightly firm, about 15 minutes.

Next,

1 box	Sugar-Free Jell-O (Same flavor as above)
2/3 cup	Lime or Raspberry Vodka
1 cup	Hot water

Boil the water and add the Jell-O, stirring constantly. After the Jell-O has dissolved, stir for another 2 minutes, then add the vodka. Stir for about a minute then pour 1/2" deep on top of the previous Jell-O. Allow to set-up until firm. Serve and enjoy!

This fun recipe can also be made using a 9"x13" baking pan. The pan needs to be at least 2" deep. Pour the Jell-O in layers, allowing each layer to set slightly before pouring the next round. Cut into 1-1/2" squares. Serve cold.

"So I said to the manager..."

"Sorry I'm late. I couldn't find my way to work." (She had been employed at the bar for more than three years.)

"I can't come in to work, my nails are wet."

"I can't come in to work today. I'm in jail, for a DUI. Is that a problem?" (He worked as a driver's education instructor.)

Responsible Bartending

As people change their eating habits, it can significantly affect the way their systems respond to alcohol. This puts more pressure on you. As a bartender, you have a substantial amount of responsibility to make sure your patrons enjoy themselves in a safe and legal manner.

A lot of people don't understand that eating a low cal, low carb salad and then slamming a couple of shots will hit their systems a lot harder then if they had just eaten a full meal with bread and meat. Extra care needs to be exercised when serving customers who are on any type of diet.

Always serve responsibly.

Don't let customers drive drunk.

"*Low carb*" means less carbohydrates, not less alcohol.

"*Lite*" or "*light*" means lower calories, not less alcohol.

It's up to you to say "when."

Check ID.

Know your state's legal drinking age,
and never serve to a minor.

This chapter is based on the training materials used to qualify individuals for the Permit to Serve Alcohol (commonly called the Mixology or Bartender License), for the state of Washington.

This chapter contains general information and is not intended to be all-inclusive. Please check with your manager or local liquor board for laws that apply to your particular state or city.

- **Never Overserve**. For most states, it is illegal to serve a person who is obviously intoxicated. This means, if the person walks into your bar, and they have already had too much, you cannot legally serve him/her. Not even one drink. Coffee, soda, other non-alcoholic drinks can, and should be encouraged.

  Should the person leave? Most of the time, there is no reason for them to leave your bar, as long as he/she is:

  1. Not acting in a manner that is dangerous to others (such as picking fights, hitting people, or making threats).

  2. Not sleeping. People in your bar must remain AWAKE.

  3. Not acting obnoxious, cussing, throwing things, or in general, making you and everyone else crazy.

  4. Keeping their clothes on.

  Try to prevent anyone who is drunk from leaving, especially if they will be driving. Offer to call a cab, call a friend, or one of their family members. Try to get the person to eat something, or have some coffee.

How can you tell if some is drunk?

Follow the **PuBS** rule:

1. **Physical changes** – Watch for stumbling, dropping things, inability to count change, lighting the wrong end of the cigarette, knocking over drinks, glassy eyes, etc.

2. **Behavioral changes** – While some people become moody and withdrawn, other become loud, boisterous, or even violent. Some may start picking fights, complaining about their friends, or the service they are receiving.

3. **Speech** – Are they slurring their words, forgetting what they are talking about, or talking in a rambling and nonsensical manner?

4. **And the "U"?** That stands for YOU, using good judgment and common sense.

Not everyone will show every symptom. But, virtually everyone will show at least one or more. If in doubt, you will need to use your own judgment. Try to watch how many drinks a person is consuming, and in what period of time. Especially watch out for doubles and "high octane" drinks like Exotics and Long Island Ice Teas – which have 2 to 2-1/2 ounces of liquor in each one. Exotics taste good, and people often drink them quickly without realizing how much liquor they have consumed.

Remember: **There is a time lag from the time a person consumes the drink, until they start exhibiting signs of intoxication.** This is why a person can drink a couple of shots in the car, walk into your bar, have a cup of coffee, and fall off the barstool. The liquor simply needed time to catch up.

- **Other serving facts to keep in mind:**

A 12-ounce bottle of beer, a 6-ounce glass of wine, and a 1-ounce shot of 86 proof liquor, all contain about the same amount of alcohol.

Does that surprise you? Most people *assume* that beer and wine have lower alcohol contents then "hard" liquor.

1. *Anyone* can become intoxicated on *any* liquor – if they drink enough of it.

2. Factors that can cause one person to become intoxicated faster then another can include:

   a. **Weight**. Heavier or overweight people are often able to drink more than a slender person before exhibiting signs of intoxication.

   b. **Gender**. Women tend to become intoxicated faster then men, on less alcohol.

   c. **Muscle mass**. The more muscular the person, the more they can generally drink before showing signs of intoxication.

   d. **How long since their last meal**. Food slows down the absorption of alcohol by the body, allowing a person to drink more, without showing signs of intoxication.

3. The average person can process about **1 ounce of hard liquor an hour.**

Only TIME will allow a person to sober up.
Coffee and fresh air can wake the person up, but only TIME will allow the alcohol to process out of their body.

- **Cutting someone off**. When you have determined that a person needs to be "cut off" (not served any more liquor for that day), here are some helpful rules to follow:

1. **Never back down.** Be firm, but polite, and offer other non-alcoholic beverages and food. Be hospitable and friendly, but stand your ground.

2. **Alert other servers.** Often a person that has been cut off will try to get a drink from other servers or other patrons.

3. **Avoid getting into an argument.** Stay calm, and avoid comments, generalizations, name-calling or making remarks that could be inflammatory, especially comments regarding gender, race or a person's parentage.

4. **Gossip:** Avoid talking about that person behind their back to other patrons.

5. **Refer to posted signs.** If your bar has signs posted stating "it is illegal to serve someone who is intoxicated," point to those signs and use that as a way to back up what you are saying.

6. **Cameras:** Simply remind the customer that everything that happens is being recorded. This also works well to help control drug dealing in your bar.

- **Drinking and Driving:** Know your state's laws regarding drinking and driving, including the blood alcohol levels for DUI and other possible legal infractions. In the State of Washington, the BAC (Blood Alcohol Concentration) for a DUI "Driving Under the Influence," conviction is .08, and .05 for "Driving While Impaired."

  Statistically, people with a BAC of .05 or higher have a 300-400% higher risk of being involved in an accident.

  In the state of Washington, 280 people a year die in alcohol related accidents. For every one of those 5 others are injured.

  If a person you served leaves your bar and is involved in an accident, both you and the bar can be held liable. It is called **Third Party Liability**.

- **Time of Service**: Know your state's times to legally serve alcohol. Some jurisdictions may have different times. Be sure you check on this. For many states, 2 a.m. is the cut off, and service can start again at 6 a.m.

- **Minors**: **It is illegal to serve minors alcohol**. Know your state's drinking age, and follow it. You can be held criminally responsible if you are caught serving a minor. This carries even more impact when you consider that **10-20% of the traffic accidents involving alcohol are caused by underage drinkers.**

- **Drinking and Drugs**: Using drugs with alcohol can compound (increase) the effect of the drug. This is true regardless if the drugs are prescription, over the counter, or illegal street drugs. It is possible for very dangerous and toxic reactions to occur.

  Mixing antihistamine, commonly taken for allergies, with alcohol can be dangerous. Many cold remedies say they help you feel better and get a good night's sleep. Ever tried one? They can knock you out for a couple days. While this is great to help you get over a cold, it can be dangerous if you are driving. Take a look at the label, you will find alcohol and antihistamine.

  Decongestants can make a person sick to their stomach when mixed with alcohol, especially red wines.

  Some street drugs can be deadly when combined with alcohol. Be especially watchful for "club drugs," like Ecstasy.

  Drugs that are depressants such as Marijuana, can make a person act much more depressed, "out of it," lost, or confused when mixed with alcohol.

  Drugs that are stimulants such as Cocaine, can make a person extremely irritable, hyperactive, or edgy, and can cause extreme mood swings when mixed with even a slight amount of alcohol.

  Although many people don't realize it, alcohol is a depressant. This explains why a person who is already upset may become much more so after a couple of drinks.

  The exhilaration people sometimes feel when drinking is caused by the increased sugar to the system, and the effect alcohol has the brain's center of inhibition.

The most common *depressant* in America is alcohol. The most common *stimulant* is caffeine.

- **Alcohol and Pregnancy**: In most states, it is ILLEGAL to refuse service to a pregnant woman, it is considered discrimination. You can make other suggestions, such as juice, coffee or a non-alcoholic drink, but you can't refuse to serve her, based on the pregnancy alone. Most states require signs to be posted alerting customers to the dangers of drinking while pregnant, including the risk of Fetal Alcohol Syndrome.

Notes to Keep Handy

I work in the State of: ______________________________

The legal drinking age for my state is: _________________

The legal BAC for driving **IMPAIRED** is: _____________

The legal BAC for driving **DRUNK** is: ________________

I can serve liquor between the hours of: _____ and ______

Source:

Washington State Liquor Control Board, *Handbook for Liquor Licensees*, 2004.

Bartending Terms

- ***Absolut*** – A popular brand of Swedish vodka. Absolut comes in a variety of flavors such as: Citron (lemon), Mandarin (orange) and Kurrent (blackberry).

- **Against the Wall** – A drink that is topped with 1/2 ounce of ***Galliano***. For example, a "*Slow Screw against the wall.*"

- ***Akvavit*** **(Aquavit)** – A caraway and rye flavored liqueur (similar to vodka) commonly served in Scandinavian communities. It is best served chilled, with a beer chaser.

- **Amaretto** – An almond or cherry flavored liqueur. Amaretto is especially popular in coffee drinks.

- ***B&B*** – Brandy and Benedictine.

- **Back** – A drink on the side, such as coffee or Coke. Commonly referred to by the name of the side drink. For example, a "*coffee back*" or a "*Coke back.*" The back is served so the patron can alternate between two drinks. Always offer a back with brandy, cognac, and straight shots.

  Customers are not normally charged for the back when it is served with an alcoholic drink, unless the back is also alcoholic. For example, a "*shot of whiskey with a beer back.*" See also **Chaser.**

- **Bank** – A specific amount of money given to the bartender for the cash register. This cash is used for making change, and must be returned at the end of the shift.

- **Bar Back (Porter)** – A person who stocks the bar with ice, beer, liquors, and supplies. A good bar back is invaluable during rush times. Always remember to tip your bar back.

- **Bar Time** – Most bars have their clocks set 15-20 minutes ahead of the actual time. This allows a few extra minutes at closing time to clear the bar of customers, without being in violation of the state liquor serving laws.

  The bar will schedule your shifts based on BAR TIME, so be sure to set your watch ahead to match it, or you will be late for work.

- **Benedictine** – A liqueur with a strong herbal flavor, made from a variety of herbs and spices, including vanilla, nutmeg and cloves.

- **Bite Me** – A humorous term used when you want to swear at someone, but not come across with the same impact as using straight profanity. It is sort of the verbal equivalent of flipping someone off.

- **Bitters** – Syrup with a strong clove flavor, made from a combination of herbs and spices. Bitters are very strong, and are used to give an herbal flavor to some exotic drinks and an "*Old Fashioned.*"

  Bitters also have medicinal value. A few drops on a lime wedge can help stop hiccups, and a few drops in Ginger Ale or Coke can help calm seasickness and morning sickness.

- **Blended** – A drink made in a blender. For example, a "*blended margarita.*"

- **Blended** – A specific type of liquor made from a combination of similar liquors. For example, a "*blended whiskey.*"

  A blended whiskey may be made up of as many as 75 different types of whiskey bases (80-125 proof) and spirits (liquors above 190 proof). Each whiskey base is aged a different amount of time. The final whiskey is built by layering the different bases and spirits and allowing them to combine over time. This combining process is known as aging.

- **Bourbon** – A special type of whiskey, made from at least 51% corn, and distilled in Bourbon County, Kentucky. Bourbon is stored in new charred barrels after distilling, and is aged at least 2 years.

- **Brandy** – Brandy is a special family of liquors. These liquors have an alcohol base, which comes from grape wine, and is often mixed with a variety of fruits and berries. The result is a very flavorful liquor that can be quite strong, sometimes as high as 84 proof.

  Brandies tend to be regional in production, based on the available fruits in the area.

  For the label to read "*Brandy*," the liquor must be made solely from grapes. If other fruits are added, the type or types must be included in the label name, for example, "*Peach Brandy*" or "*Apricot Brandy.*"

  Brandies are aged in oak barrels for 3-8 years.

- **Bruised** – A drink that has been shaken with ice, rather then stirred, and served in a chilled glass. This term usually refers to a Martini or a Manhattan.

- **Bucket Glass** – A medium size, wide mouth glass that holds about 10 ounces of liquid.

- **Bud** – ***Budweiser Beer***. A popular American beer.

- **CC** – ***Canadian Club*** whiskey. Also short for credit card.

- ***Chambord*** – A liqueur with a strong raspberry or grape flavor, used in making Grape Nehis and Black Opals.

- **Chaser** – A drink on the side, such as coffee or Coke. Commonly referred to by the name of the side drink. For example, a "*coffee chaser*" or a "*Coke chaser.*" The chaser is served so the patron can alternate between two drinks. Always offer a chaser with brandy, cognac, and straight shots.

Customers are not normally charged for the chaser when it is served with an alcoholic drink, unless it is also alcoholic. For example, a *"shot of whiskey with a beer chaser."* The term "chaser" is more common in an upscale restaurant then in a nightclub or sports bar. See also **Back**.

- **Chiller** – The air conditioner.

- **Club Soda** – A flavorless, carbonated mixer, also referred to as soda water.

> Some cities, particularly on the East Coast, refer to cola (Coke) as "soda." When mixing drinks, soda refers to SODA WATER or CLUB SODA. When in doubt, ask your customer which they mean.

- **Cocktail** – A mixed drink. Also a term for a cocktail waitress or waiter.

- **Cognac** – A brandy distilled in Cognac, France. Some of the most popular include ***Courvoisier***, ***Remy Martin***, and ***Hennessy***.

- ***Cointreau*** – An orange flavored liqueur.

- **Colorado Bulldog** – The same drink as a Smith and Wesson. Colorado Bulldog is a popular name for the drink in the Midwest, while Smith and Wesson tends to be more common on the West Coast.

- **Cooler** – The large refrigerated storage area for restaurant food supplies and beer kegs.

- **Crème de** – Liqueurs made with fruits, berries and sometimes nuts. These sweet liqueurs are often used in exotic drinks or shooters. Some of the most common:

- **Crème de Almond (Noyaux)** – A liqueur with a fruit punch flavor, used in a wide variety of exotic drinks, including Hurricanes, Mai Tais, and Zombies.
- **Crème de Banana** – A liqueur with a light banana and pineapple flavor.
- **Crème de Cacao** – A chocolate flavored liqueur. This liqueur comes in two different colors, white (clear), or brown, and is common in coffee drinks and shooters.
- **Crème de Coconut** – A liqueur with a strong coconut flavor, used in exotic drinks such as Pina Coladas and Bahama Mamas. This liqueur is very popular in drinks served in resorts, and Asian and Mexican restaurants.
- **Crème de Menthe** – A peppermint flavored liqueur. Crème de Menthe comes in two colors, white (clear) and green.
- **Crème de Café** – A coffee flavored liqueur.
- **Crème de Cassis** – A liqueur has a strong black current flavor.

- **Crown** – ***Crown Royal*** Canadian whiskey.
- ***Curacao*** – An orange flavored liqueur, made on the Island of Curacao. Usually blue, it may come in a variety of other colors.

  Blue ***Curacao*** is used in making exotic drinks such as Blue Hawaiians and Blue Margaritas.
- **Cut Off** – A patron who is not allowed to have any more liquor for that day. Food, coffee, and cola may be recommended as alternatives.

- **Dirty** – A drink served with 1/4-1/2 ounce green olive juice poured into it. This term is most often used in connection with Martinis.

- **Draft** – Tap beer, served in a chilled glass.

- ***Drambuie*** – A brand of Scottish liqueur with the flavors of heather and honey.

- **Double** – Double the amount of liquor, but serve it in the same size glass. This gives a very strong drink, with just a little mixer. For example, a *"double rum and Coke"* means 2 ounces of rum and a little Coke in a bucket glass.

- **86'ed** – A patron who has become so unruly that they are barred from coming back into the bar. The barring may be temporary or permanent.

- **Electric** – A drink that is topped with 1/2 ounce of tequila. For example, an "*Electric Ice Tea.*"

- **English** – A drink that is topped with 1/2 ounce of gin. For example, a "*vodka and tonic with a little English.*"

- **First Call** – The notification a bartender gives guests to let them know the bar is now open to serve alcohol (usually 6 am).

- **Flair** – Serving drinks with an exceptional skill and showmanship delivery. May including fancy ways of popping tops off beer bottles, flipping and catching (the operative word here is – CATCH) bottles and glasses, even flipping and tossing fruit and ice.

  ** Practice flair techniques at home before you try them at work. Don't try to show off too much. Better to simply serve customers well, then miss a catch and break several expensive bottles of liquor.

- **Flaming** – Drinks with a high alcohol content, which are lit, and then served while on fire.

> ***Note: In most states, flaming drinks are illegal to serve.***

- **Float** – The top 1/2-ounce of liquor or syrup "floated" on top of a drink, for example, a "*rum and Coke® with a float of Grenadine*." A float may also be referred to as a top, or a lid.

  Depending on the liquor, other terms may apply, such as screaming (vodka), electric (tequila), English (gin), multiple (***Frangelico***), and against the wall (***Galliano***).

- ***Frangelico*** – A hazelnut flavored Italian liqueur, packaged in a distinctive bottle shaped like a monk, complete with a rope belt.

- **Free Pouring** – A method professional bartenders use to measure liquor by counting or "feeling" when an ounce has been poured. Good bartenders can free pour accurately with both hands simultaneously. Special pour spouts to control liquor flow from the bottle are normally used.

- ***Galliano*** – A brand of licorice and vanilla flavored liqueur, sold in a distinctive, long neck bottle. The neck is so long that bartenders tend to knock over the bottle when they reach for nearby liquors. As a precaution, Galliano® is stored against the wall. This explains the term "Against the Wall," which means to add Galliano® to a drink.

- **Gin** – Liquor similar to whiskey, which has been flavored with Juniper berries.

- **Gold** ***(Golden)*** – The term "gold" usually refers to tequila that has been aged in oak whiskey barrels. For example, ***Jose Cuervo Gold.***

"Gold" may also refer to a drink made with gold tequila, such as a Gold Margarita.

- ***<u>Goldschlager</u>*** – A Swiss cinnamon liqueur that contains distinctive 24 karat gold flakes. ***Goldschlager*** is normally served chilled, and should be shaken to float the gold flakes.
  This liqueur is often used in shooters and coffee drinks.

- ***<u>Grand Marnier</u>*** – A French liqueur with strong orange flavors. ***Grand Marnier*** is often served heated.

- **<u>Grenadine</u>** – A non-alcoholic cherry flavored syrup made from pomegranates.

- **<u>Head</u>** – The foamy top of a beer.

- **<u>Head</u>** – A slang or street term for the restroom.

- **<u>Heat</u>** – Local police, liquor control board officers, or any undercover federal or county police officer. "The Heat's in the house," usually means Liquor Control is in the bar. As always, be sure to check ID on everyone.

- **<u>Heater</u>** – A bucket, or similar glass, filled with very hot water, and served with a snifter of brandy or cognac. The customer lays the snifter on top of the bucket glass to warm the brandy. Serve a fresh heater with each new brandy ordered.

> **Advise your cocktail person that the glass is HOT, as they may pick it up when serving and get burned, or not expect a hot glass and drop it.**

- **<u>Heferweizen</u>** ***(Hef)*** – A popular German style beer. Heferweizen is a thick, unfiltered beer that is slightly fruity tasting, and is served with lemon wedges.

- **<u>Holy Water</u>** – ***Christian Brothers*** Brandy.

- **Hurt Me** – A customer's request to pour the liquor a little extra heavy. For example, a "*gin and tonic, and hurt me.*"

  "Hurt me" is a different term then "bite me," which is the verbal equivalent of flipping you off.

- **Irish Cream** - A chocolate and cream flavored liqueur made with an Irish whiskey base. Irish cream is especially popular in coffee drinks and shooters.

- ***Jagermeister*** - A popular German liqueur with the flavors of licorice and rootbeer.

- **Jigger** – An hourglass shaped measuring device, usually steel. The most common type measures 1 ounce on one side and 1 1/2 ounces on the other. Other measurements are available.

- ***Kahlua*** – A coffee flavored liqueur made in Mexico. ***Kahlua*** is very popular in coffee drinks and shooters. ***Kapali*** is the brand name of a similar, lower cost product.

- **Keg** – A metal container for holding tap beer. Full size kegs may weigh as much as 300 pounds. Smaller kegs are called Pony Kegs.

  Kegs must be kept cold. If the beer is allowed to get warm the flavor may change, and it will result in foamy pouring.

- **Kosher** – Products made following Jewish laws, and blessed by a Rabbi.

- **Last Call** – The notification, usually yelled across the bar or announced over the loud speaker, that a bartender gives guests to let them know it is getting close to closing time, or the time when they must stop serving alcohol. Customers are allowed to order one last drink. Some bars announce Last Call about half and hour before they have to pull the drinks, others may give Last Call as close as 10 – 15 minutes before closing.

- **Loaded** – A customer that has had too much to drink. Women may be referred to as "tipsy" (generally this would be said of an older woman), while men are generally referred to as loaded, smashed, lit or overdone.

- **Lid** – The 1/2-oz of liquor or syrup floated on top of a drink. The lid is often a contrasting color to the main drink, and is added for both taste and appearance. For example, a Mai Tai is made with a dark brown lid of ***Myers'*** rum.

  A lid may also be referred to as a top or a float. Depending on the liquor other terms may apply, such as screaming (vodka), electric (tequila), English (gin), multiple (***Frangelico***), and against the wall (***Galliano***).

- **Light** – A match or cigarette lighter.

- **Light** – Serving a cocktail with slightly less alcohol then the drink normally requires. For example, a "*rum and Coke - light.*"

- **Liqueur** – Liqueurs or cordials, are made using a straight liquor base such as whiskey, gin or vodka, and distilling them with fruits, berries, nuts, flowers, twigs, etc. The result is a very flavorful, high sugar content liquor.

- **Mexican** – A drink topped with 1/2 ounce of tequila. For example, a "*Fuzzy Naval Mexican Style.*"

- **Microbrewery** – Small, local breweries.

- ***Midori*** – A Japanese liqueur with the flavor of honeydew melon.

- **Multiple** – A drink topped with 1/2 ounce of ***Frangelico***. For example, a "*multiple Smith and Wesson.*"

- **Neat** – A drink served at room temperature with no ice.

- **151** – A high proof type of rum. 151 is highly flammable, and is often used in flaming drinks.

> ***In most states, flaming drinks are illegal to serve.***

- ***Ouzo*** – A Greek liqueur with a strong licorice flavor. ***Ouzo*** is normally served chilled.

- **Permit to Serve Alcohol** (Over the Age of 21). This is a license granted by the State Liquor Control Board to allow bartenders, waiters and waitresses to mix, pour, and serve alcohol. It requires that you be **21 years of age or older**, (or the legal drinking age in your state.) You must take a class provided by a state-licensed instructor, and be tested on your knowledge of the state laws and regulations. The permit is valid for 5 years, and must be renewed prior to that time by retaking the class and re-testing. The permit can be revoked for violations of state laws, including DUI or drug related convictions, and serving violations - especially serving to minors.

- **Permit to Serve Alcohol** (Under 21 years of age). This is a license granted by the State Liquor Control Board to allow waiters and waitresses to *serve alcohol,* **(you are NOT allowed to mix or pour drinks, or act as a bartender).** It requires that you to be 18-21 years of age, (check with your particular State's laws). You must take a class provided by a state-licensed instructor, and be tested on your knowledge of the state laws and regulations. The permit is valid until you reach the age of 21. When you reach 21, you can automatically upgrade to the license designated for those over 21. Your permit can be revoked for violations of state laws, including DUI or drug related convictions, and serving violations - especially serving to minors.

- **Port Wine** – A sweet, dessert-type wine that has been fortified with brandy.

- **Pounder** – The large, heavy glass used to serve draft beer. This glass is called a "pounder," because it holds 16 ounces, or a "pound" of beer.

- **Press** – Short for "Presbyterian," a mixed drink made of liquor and a mixture of 1/2 Ginger Ale and 1/2 soda water.

- **Quinine Water** – Carbonated water containing a small amount of Quinine. Quinine water is also known as tonic water, and has a characteristic slightly bitter taste.

  Tonic water was originally used in the East Indies to fight Malaria.

  Tonic water is usually labeled on a speed gun as "Q," for Quinine.

- **Rocks** – Ice.

- **Rocks Glass** – A small glass used to serve 1 to 1 1/2 shot drinks, over ice (rocks). This glass holds about 5 ounces total.

- **Rose's Lime Juice** – A non-alcoholic lime flavored syrup, used in a variety of drinks, such as margaritas and Kamikazes.

- ***Rumpleminze*** - A high quality peppermint schnapps made in Germany.

- ***Sambuca*** – A licorice flavored Italian liqueur. ***Sambuca*** is normally served chilled.

- **Schnapps** – German style liqueurs that come in a wide variety of flavors, including peppermint, peach, apricot and blackberry.

- **Schooner** – A large, tulip shaped glass used in serving draft beer. A schooner holds about 16 ounces. Smaller versions are called Half Schooners.
- **Screaming** – A drink topped with 1/2 ounce of vodka. For example, a "*screaming Melon Ball.*"
- **Shift** – A scheduled time for working.
- **Short** – A drink served in a smaller glass than is normally used. This gives a stronger drink, because of the reduced amount of mixer.
- **Short Shot** – Serving a cocktail or shot with slightly less alcohol then the drink normally requires. Short shots are usually charged at full price.
- **Shot** – A measurement equivalent to one ounce.
- **Shot Glass** – The small glass used to serve a straight shot of liquor.
- **Skimming** – A slang term for stealing from the cash register.
- **Sloe Gin** – A liqueur made from Sloeberries, a berry similar to a raspberry. There is no gin in Sloe Gin.
- **Snifter** – The bowl shaped glass used to serve brandy and cognac.
- ***SoCo*** – ***Southern Comfort*** liqueur.
- **Soda** – A flavorless, carbonated mixer, also referred to as club soda.

> Some cities, particularly on the East Coast, refer to cola (Coke) as "soda." When mixing drinks, soda refers to **SODA WATER** or **CLUB SODA**. When in doubt, ask your customer which they mean.

- ***Southern Comfort*** (***SoCo***) – A popular brand of liqueur with the flavors of apricot and peaches.

- **Splash** – A squirt of requested item, about 1/2 ounce, added on top of the drink. For example, a "*gin and tonic with a splash of 7-up.*"

- **Splash** – A non-alcoholic blend of fruit juices and 7-Up, served over ice in a large glass.

- **Spritzer** – A light, refreshing drink made from a combination of 1/2 wine (any type, especially flavored wines) or champagne, and 1/2 club soda. A Spritzer is served in a tall glass, over ice.

  Some popular combinations include a White Wine Spritzer (made with White Zinfandel), a Red Wine Spritzer (made with Merlot or Cabernet Sauvignon).

  For a sweeter drink, try a Red Wine Spritzer made with port wine, or a 1/2 shot of brandy or other flavored liqueur.

- **Squeeze** – A technique for adding fruit juice to a drink.

- ***Stoli*** – ***Stolichnaya*** Vodka, a popular Russian vodka that comes in a variety of flavors. Some of the most popular are vanilla and raspberry.

- **Straight Up** – A drink that has been shaken or stirred with ice to chill it then served in a chilled glass, with no ice.

- **Tab** – A bar bill a customer may run for drinks and food. Most bars require the customer to secure the bill with a credit card.

- **Tall** – A drink served in a glass larger then the drink is normally served in. This means the drink has a less intense alcohol flavor because of the additional mixer.

- **Tequila** – A liquor made primarily in Mexico, from the distilled sap of the Blue Agave plant, which is similar to a cactus. In America, we know this plant as the American Aloe. To be called tequila, the liquor must be distilled near the city of Tequila, Mexico. Tequilas made elsewhere in Mexico are called Mescal.

  Tequila can be sold aged or unaged. Aged tequilas such as ***Jose Cuervo Gold***, and ***Cuervo 1800*** are matured in used whiskey barrels, resulting in a mellower flavor and a soft golden color.

- ***Tia Maria*** – A coffee flavored Jamaican liqueur, similar to ***Kahlua***.

- **Till** – The cash register.

- **Tip** – A payment made by a customer to a bartender or server in appreciation of service.

  Remember: customers are not required to tip you. You need to EARN the tip with good service and a positive attitude.

- **Tonic Water** – Carbonated water containing a small amount of Quinine. Tonic water is also known as Quinine water, and has a characteristic slightly bitter taste.

  Tonic water was originally used in the East Indies to fight Malaria.

  Tonic water is usually labeled on a speed gun as "Q," for Quinine.

- **Top** – The 1/2-ounce of liquor or syrup floating on top of a drink. For example, a "*rum and Coke topped with Grenadine*."

A top may also be referred to as a lid, or a float. Depending on the liquor, other terms may apply, such as screaming (vodka), electric (tequila), English (gin), multiple (***Frangelico***), and against the wall (***Galliano***).

- **Topless** – A drink served without a salted or sugared rim. For example, a "*topless Bloody Mary*."
- **Training Wheels** – The lemon slices served with tequila.
- **Triple Sec** – An orange flavored liqueur, used in a wide variety of drinks from Exotics to margaritas and Long Island ice teas. Triple Sec is usually found in the "well" or speed rack.
- ***Tuaca*** – An Italian liqueur with the flavors of caramel, vanilla, and fruit.
- **Turkey** – ***Wild Turkey*** bourbon
- **Unleaded** – A term that usually refers to decaffeinated coffee. When talking about a drink, it means a drink made with no alcohol.
- **Up** – Short for ***Straight Up***, a drink that has been shaken or stirred with ice to chill it, then served in a chilled glass, with no ice.
- **Velvet** – ***Black Velvet*** Canadian whiskey.
- **Virgin** – A drink made with no alcohol.
- **Well** – The bartender's ice bin.

- **Well Drinks** – Cheap drinks made from house liquors. These cheaper liquors are stored in the rack beside or in front of the "well" (the bartender's ice bin).

- **Well Speed Rack** – The shelf the house liquors are kept in for fast drink mixing. The rack (or shelf) is set directly in front of, or beside the bartender's ice bin.

- ***Yukon Jack*** – A popular Canadian liqueur, often miscategorized as a whiskey. Yukon is considered a liqueur due to a very high sugar content.

- **Zin** – Short for Zinfandel wine.

A Few Last Thoughts

I hope that you have found this book to be both helpful and entertaining. Take heart fellow bartenders! Together, we will meet the challenges of our changing world.

As you go forth, here is a little bartender humor for you.

Trouble Ahead

Just when customers start tipping,
More than is fitting,

The waitstaff stops fighting,
And a smoke you are lighting,

The boss calls in with a cold,
(Or so you are told),

But it's going so well,
You say, "What the hell?"

A favor he needs, and so you agree,
To work his shift too, ***how bad could it be?***

Happy bartending!

Sources Consulted

"Absolut Vodka," *Drinksmixer.com,* <http://www.drinksmixer.com/desc136.html>, (10 June 2004).

Adams, Cecil, "Will the quinine in tonic water prevent malaria?" *The Straight Dope, a division of Chicago Reader, Inc.*, 13 August 1999, <http://www.straightdope.com/classics/a990813.html>, (21 April 2004).

Agatston, Arthur, *The South Beach Diet: The Delicious, Doctor-Designed, Foolproof Plan for Fast and Healthy Weight Loss*, Rodale Books, 2003.

"Alcohol and Your Low Carb Diet," reprinted article from www.lowcarbluxury.com, *Low-carb.com*, <http://www.low-carb.com/article-03.html>, (10 June 2004).

"Amaretto Di Saronno," *Drinksmixer.com,* <http://www.drinksmixer.com/desc154.html>, (10 June 2004).

Atkins, Dr. Robert C., *Dr. Atkins' New Carbohydrate Gram Counter,* M. Evans and Company, 1997.

Atkins, Dr. Robert C., *Dr. Atkins' New Diet Revolution*, Avon Books, 2001.

"Bailey's Irish Cream," *Drinksmixer.com,* <http://www.drinksmixer.com/desc191.html>, (10 June 2004).

"Bacardi to buy Grey Goose vodka. Deal gives company first major vodka brand," *MSNBNC News,* <http://msnbc.msn.com/id/5256874/>, (25 June 2004).

"Bacardi to buy Grey Goose vodka," *BBC News – World Edition*, 21 June, 2004, <http://news.bbc.co.uk/2/hi/business/3825287.stm>, (25 June 2004).

"Baja Bob's Low Carb Drink Mixes," *Netrition.com,* <http://www11.netrition.com/baja_bobs_mix_page.html>, (10 June 2004)

"Beer and Your Health. Calories, Carbs and Alcohol," *Realbeer.com*, <http://www.realbeer.com/edu/health/calories.php>, (12 June 2004).

"Blue Curacao," *Drinksmixer.com,* <http://www.drinks mixer.com/desc1366.html>, (10 June 2004).

"Beefeater Gin," *Thomas Lowndes & Co. Ltd.* (a subsidiary of Allied Domecq Spirits & Wine Ltd.), <http://www.thomas lowndes.com/beefeater.html>, (4 April 2004).

"Can I Drink Alcohol While on Atkins?," Everything Atkins.net, <http://www.everythingatkins.net/atkinsfaqs.html>, (10 June 2004).

"Carb Counter," *Carb-counter.org,* <http://www.carb-counter.org>, (5 June 2004).
**** This is a great reference site for food as well as drink combinations. I found it quite easy to use.**

"Carbohydrate Counter," *Lowcarbfriends.com*, <http://forum.lowcarbfriends.com/carbcounter/bev. shtml>, (14 June 2004)
**** This is an excellent reference site, and easy to use.**

"Carbohydrate Counts of Common Foods," *Diabetes.about.com*, <http://diabetes.about.com/cs/carbcentral/l/blcarbsA.htm>, (10 June 2004).
**** This is an excellent reference site, and easy to use.**

"Carbohydrates in Soft Drinks," *Anne Collins Diet, Annecollins.com,* <http://www.annecollins.com/ dietary-carbs/carbs-soft-drinks.htm>, (10 June 2004).

"Chambord Raspberry Liqueur," *Drinksmixer.com,* <http://www. Drinksmixer.com/desc247.html>, (10 June 2004).

"Christian Brothers Brandy," *Drinksmixer.com,* <http://www. drinksmixer.com/desc912.html>, (2 June 2004).

"Clydesdale Stables, Grant's Farm," *Anheuser-Busch Inc*., <http://www.grantsfarm.com/docs/stables.htm>, (1 May 2004).

"Cocktails," *Low-Carb and Loving it, Lowcarbhelp.homestead.com* <http://lowcarbhelp. homestead.com/cocktails.html>, (2 June 2004).

"Coors Brewing Company: Celebrating 125 Years of Brewing Excellence," *Rocky Mountain Beer Notes*, April 1998, <http://www.beernotes.com/rockymtn/ articles/ 000324.html>, (04 April 2004).

"Coors Organization/History," *Birmingham Beverage Company*, <http://www.alabev.com/coorsorg.htm>, (04 April 2004).

"Courvoisier Cognac," *Drinksmixer.com,* <http://www. drinksmixer.com/desc928.html>, (10 June 2004).

"Crystal Light Product Information," *Kraftfoods.com,* <http://www.kraftfoods.com/crystallight/cl_products.html>, (15 June 2004)

"Drink Like 007," *M16 – The Home of 007*, 26th November 2002, <http://www.mi6.co.uk/sections/ articles/drink_ like_007.php3?t=&s=articles>, (5 May 2004).

If you are a James Bond fan, you absolutely must see this site.

"E & J Brandy," *Drinksmixer.com,* <http://www.drinks mixer.com/desc949.html>, (10 June 2004).

"Famous Budweiser Clydesdales," *Budweiser Company, a division of Anheuser-Busch Inc.*, <http://www.budweiser tours.com/docs/clydes.htm>, (2 May 2004).

"Flavored Rums," *Drinksmixer.com,* <http://www.drinks mixer.com/desc799.html>, (10 June 2004).

"Frangelico Hazelnut Liqueur," *Drinksmixer.com,* <http:// www.drinksmixer.com/desc285.html>, (10 June 2004).,

"Gin," *Drinksmixer.com,* <http://www.drinksmixer. com/desc5.html, (10 June 2004).
**** This is a great reference site.**

"Gin and Tonic," *Science Daily LLC*, <http://www. Science daily.com/encyclopedia/gin_and_tonic>, (2 April 2004).

GNS, "Rum Lords: History of Bacardi Terror," *Hindustan Times Ltd*, 13 April, <http://www.hindustantimes.com/news/ 5922_680719,0015002100000 121.htm>, (30 April 2004)

"Goldschlager," *Drinksmixer.com,* <http://www.drinks mixer.com/desc527.html>, (10 June 2004).

"Grand Marnier," *Drinksmixer.com,* <http://www.drinks mixer.com/desc532.html>, (10 June 2004).

"Hennessy Cognac," *Drinksmixer.com,* <http://www. drinksmixer.com/desc696.html>, (10 June 2004).

Howard, Theresa, "Atkins Diet Inspires Low Carb Beers," *USAToday.com*, <http://www.usatoday.com/ money /industries/ food/2003-08-21-lowcarb_x.htm>, (10 June 2004).

"HPNOTIQ," *Drinksmixer.com,* <http://www.drinks mixer.com/desc1332.html>, (10 June 2004).

"Jagermeister," *Drinksmixer.com,* <http://www.drinks mixer.com/desc535.html>, (10 June 2004).

"James Burrough – the Founder," *Beefeater Gin*, <http://beefeatergin.com>, (15 March 2004).

"Kahlua," *Drinksmixer.com,* <http://www.drinks mixer.com/desc292.html>, (10 June 2004).

"King of Beers – History Timeline," *Budweiser Company, a division of Anheuser-Busch Inc.*, <http://www.bud weiser.ca/kob_history.html>, (25 April 2004).

"Liqueurs," *Drinksmixer.com,* <http://www.drinks mixer.com/desc29.html>, (10 June 2004).

"Low Carb Beer," *Low Carb Resource.com*, <http://www.low carb-resource.com/low-carb-beer.html>, (12 June 2004).

"Low Carb Diets In Review," *Low Carb Resource.com*, <http://www.lowcarb-resource.com/lowcarb diets.html>, (12 June 2004).

"Low Carb Parties," *Lowcarbparties.com*, <http://www.lowcarb parties.com/index.php?s= tequila&RhRemDetails=0&RhLanguage=en&RhFlashEnable d=1&RhReferer=lowcarbparties.com&RhCountry=US&RhY ear=1963>, (10 June 2004).

"Make Mine a 007 – The James Bond Films," *The Minister of Martinis*, 2002, <http://home.earthlink.net/ ~atomic_rom/007/films.htm>, (5 May 2004).

"Malibu Coconut Rum," *Drinksmixer.com,* <http://www.drinksmixer.com/desc1.html>, (10 June 2004).

"Malibu Rum," *Diabeticgourmet.com*, <http://diabetic gourmet.com/forum/counting/index.cgi?read=1782>, (10 June 2004).

Melhoff, Craig, "Cure for what ails you? Why gin and tonic isn't covered by your medical benefits," *The National Pist*, <http://www.pist.ca/news/gin.html>, (3 April 2004).

"Midori," *Drinksmixer.com,* <http://www.drinks mixer.com/ desc303.html>, (10 June 2004).

"Myer's Dark Rum," *Drinksmixer.com,* <http://www. drinksmixer. com/desc506.html>, (10 June 2004).

Ness, Carol, "Curbing carbs. Dieters belly up to the bar for Atkins-style libations," *The San Francisco Chronicle*, March 18, 2004, <http://www.sfgate.com/ cgi-bin/article.cgi?f=/c/a/2004/03/18/WIGIQ5L TBC1.DTL>, (21 June 24, 2004).

"99 Bananas," *Drinksmixer.com,* <http://www.drinks mixer.com/desc841.html>, (10 June 2004).

"Peach Schnapps," *Drinksmixer.com,* <http://www. drinksmixer.com/desc191.html>, (10 June 2004).

"Peppermint Schnapps," *Drinksmixer.com,* <http://www. drinksmixer.com/desc1613.html>, (10 June 2004).

"Remy Martin Cognac," *Drinksmixer.com,* <http://www. drinksmixer.com/desc1112.html>, (10 June 2004).

"Rumple Minze," *Drinksmixer.com,* <http://www. drinksmixer.com/desc330.html>, (10 June 2004).

"Rums," *Drinksmixer.com,* <http://www.drinks mixer.com /desc2.html>, (10 June 2004).

Shea, Lisa "Wine, Carbohydrates and Blood Sugar Levels," *Wine.about.com*, <http://wine.about.com/ library/ weekly/aa061703.htm>, 12 June 2004).

Shea, Lisa, "Wine, Carbohydrates and the Atkins Diet," *Wine.about.com*, <http://wine.about.com/cs/recipeswith wine/a/atkins.htm>, (5 June 2004).

Shea, Lisa, "USDA Nutritional Values of Wine," *Wine.about.com*, <http://wine.about.com/cs/winemaking/a/usdawine.htm>, (5 June 2004).

"Skyy Vodka," *Drinksmixer.com,* <http://www.drinks mixer.com/desc332.html>, (10 June 2004).

"Smirnoff Vodka," *Drinksmixer.com,* <http://www.drinks mixer.com/desc137.html>, (10 June 2004).

Smith, Brian, "The History of Bacardi Rum," *PageWise, Inc*, 2002, <http://md.essortment.com/ historybacardi_rwng.htm>, (6 March 2004).

"Sour Apple Puckers," *Drinksmixer.com,* <http://www. drinksmixer.com/desc209.htm>, (10 June 2004).

"Southern Comfort," *Drinksmixer.com,* <http://www. drinksmixer.com/desc336.html>, (10 June 2004).

"Stolichnaya Vodka," *Drinksmixer.com,* <http://www. drinksmixer.com/desc326.html, (10 June 2004).

"Tequila," *Drinksmixer.com,* <http://www.drinks mixer.com/desc24.html>, (10 June 2004).

"Today, the Bacardi Bat is a welcomed character in over 170 countries worldwide," *Bacardi Worldwide*, <http://www. bacardi.ca/batorigins.asp?cityID=1&ticket=>, (5 April 2004)

"Tonic Water," *Science Daily LLC*, <http://www. Science daily.com/encyclopedia/tonic_water>, (2 April 2004).

"Triple Sec," *Drinksmixer.com,* <http://www.drink smixer.com/desc1444.html>, (10 June 2004).

"Vodka," *Drinksmixer.com,* <http://www.drinks mixer.com/desc28.html>, (10 June 2004).

Washington State Liquor Control Board, *Handbook for Liquor Licensees*, 2004.

"Watermelon Puckers," *Drinksmixer.com,* <http://www.drinksmixer.com/desc808.html>, (10 June 2004).

"Whiskey," *Drinksmixer.com,* <http://www.drinks mixer.com/desc5.html>, (10 June 2004).

"Why did James Bond want his martinis shaken, not stirred?," *The Straight Dope*, 28-Nov-2000, <http://www.straightdope.com/mailbag/mmartini.html> (5 May 2004).

"Wild Spirit," *Drinksmixer.com,* <http://www.drinks mixer.com/desc806.html>, (10 June 2004).

"Yukon Jack," *Drinksmixer.com,* <http://www.drinks mixer.com/desc552.html>, (10 June 2004).

"So I said to the manager…"

"I can't come in to work, my turtle is having puppies."

"I'm going to be late. I lost my mind, somewhere. It wasn't where I put it last night."

Additional Sources

This section is made up of a wide variety of fun and interesting web resources. For most of these sites, you must be 21 or over to enter.

Beer:

1. www.brewpubzone.com (Beer Information)
2. www.budweiser.com (Budweiser Information)
3. www.corona.com (Corona Mexican Beer)
4. www.corona-extra.net (Corona Mexican Beer)
5. www.coors.com (Coors Brewery)
6. www.millerbrewing.com (Miller Brewing Co.)
7. www.pyramidbrew.com (Pyramid Ales Brewery)
8. www.redhook.com (Red Hook Brewery)
9. www.washingtonbrewfest.com (Beer Festivals)

Brandy/Cognacs:

1. www.gallo.com (E&J Brandy)
2. www.heaven-hill.com (Christian Brothers Brandy)
3. www.hennessy-night.com (Hennessy Cognac)
4. www.remy.com (Remy Martin Cognac)

Gin:

1. www.alcoholreviews.com (Liquor Reviews)
2. www.beefeater.com (Beefeater Gin)
3. www.beefeaterlondonradio.co.uk (Beefeater Gin)
4. www.bestinwine.com (Liquor Reviews)
5. www.bombaysapphire.com (Bombay Gins)
6. www.ginvodka.org (Gin and Vodka Information)
7. www.hawksburn.co.uk (Hawksburn Gin)
8. www.perryland.com (Gin Drinkers Club for Bombay Gin Enthusiasts)

Rum:

1. www.bacardi.com (Bacardi Distilleries)
2. www.cabanaboyrum.com (Cabana Boy Rums)
3. www.gocaribbean.com (Caribbean Cruises)
4. www.missionliquors.com (Liquor Information)
5. www.mountgay.com (Mount Gay Rums)
6. www.rum.com (Captain Morgan Rum)
7. www.rum.cz (Rum Information)
8. www.thedrinkshop.com (Rum Recipes)

Tequila:

1. www.cuervo.com (Cuervo Distilleries)
2. www.ianchadwick.com (Tequila Information)
3. www.lasmargaritas.com (Margarita Information)
4. www.loscabosguide.com (Los Cabos Travel Info)
5. www.mixed-drink.com (Tequila Recipes)
6. www.theculturedtraveler.com (Travel Information)
7. www.tequila-shots.com (Tequila Recipes)
8. www.vivatequila.com (Tequila Information)

Vodka:

1. www.absolut.com (Absolut Vodka)
2. www.honeyvodka.com (Honey Vodka Information)
3. www.ivodka.com (Vodka Information)
4. www.questia.com (On-Line library)
5. www.smirnoff.com (Smirnoff Vodka)
6. www.stoli.com (Stoli Vodka)
7. www.skyy.com (Skyy Vodka)
8. www.vodkaphiles.com (Vodka Information)

Whiskey:

1. www.bushmills.com (Bushmill's Irish Whiskey)
2. www.classicwhiskey.com (Whiskey Information))
3. www.jackdaniels.com (Jack Daniel's Whiskey)
4. www.johnniewalker.com (Johnnie Walker Scotch)
5. www.scotchwhisky.com (Whiskey Information)

6. www.seagrams.com (Seagram's Distillery)
7. www.seagram7.com (Seagram's American Distillery)
8. www.vowhisky.com (Seagram's Canadian Distillery)
9. www.whisky-tours.com (Whiskey Distilleries)

Wine:

1. www.americanwineries.org (Nat Assn of Wineries)
2. www.columbiawinery.com (Columbia Crest Winery)
3. www.coveyrun.com (Covey Run Vintners)
4. www.gallo.com (Ernest & Julio Gallo Winery)
5. www.gunbun.com (Gundlach-Bundschu Winery)
6. www.inglenook.com (Inglenook Wines)
7. www.napavintners.com (Napa Valley Vintners)
8. www.silverlakewinery.com (Silverlake Winery)
9. www.ste-michelle.com (Chateau Ste. Michelle Winery)
10. www.valleywinetours.com (California winery tours)
11. www.weekendwinery.com (WA Wineries - good info)
12. www.winepressnw.com (Washington Wineries)
13. www.zinfandel.org (Zinfandel lovers site)

Other Fun Sites

1. www.baileys.com (Bailey's Irish Cream)
2. www.chambordonline.com (Chambord)
3. www.disaronno.com (Di Saronno Amaretto)
4. www.grand-marnier.com (Grand Marnier)
5. www.jager.com (Jagermeister Information)
6. www.jagermeister.com (Jagermeister Information)
7. www.kahlua.com (Kahlua Distillery)
8. www.milioni.com (Galliano recipes)
9. www.southerncomfort.com (Southern Comfort)

Favorite Drinks

Use these pages to write down fun, new drink combinations.

www.ingramcontent.com/pod-product-compliance
Lightning Source LLC
LaVergne TN
LVHW090948080826
845145LV00003B/934

* 9 7 8 0 9 7 6 2 1 9 8 0 4 *